GCSE Biology Practical Assessment

Teacher's Manual

David Newsham

Hutchinson Education

An imprint of Century Hutchinson Ltd
62–65 Chandos Place,
London WC2N 4NW

Century Hutchinson Australia Pty Ltd
89–91 Albion Street, Surry Hills,
New South Wales 2010, Australia

Century Hutchinson New Zealand Ltd
PO Box 40–086, Glenfield, Auckland 10,
New Zealand

Century Hutchinson South Africa (Pty) Ltd
PO Box 337, Bergvlei, 2012 South Africa

First Published 1988

Reprinted 1988

© David J. Newsham
Illustrations by Jeremy Newsham
Text set in $11/12\frac{1}{2}$ Cheltenham Light at
Tradespools Ltd, Frome, Somerset
Printed and bound in Great Britain
Designed by Nick Maddren

British Library Cataloguing in Publication Data
Newsham, David J.
  GCSE biology practical assessment.
  Teacher's guide
  1. Biology
  574 QH308

  ISBN 0 09 173142 9

Preface

Aim 1 of the *GCSE National Criteria for Science* underlines the importance of regular and relevant experimental work in all the science disciplines:

> To provide through well-designed studies of experimental and practical science a worthwhile educational experience for all pupils whether or not they go on to study science beyond this level and, in particular, to enable them to acquire sufficient understanding and knowledge.

The practical nature of all biology courses is further stressed in the *GCSE National Criteria for Biology* which requires that experimental and observational work should pervade the four Themes of the Core Content.

In both respects, the teaching of GCSE biology is no different to what teaching other biology syllabuses has been, in my experience, for the last 25 years. Where practical aspects of GCSE biology differ is that the skills pupils have always had to acquire in performing laboratory investigations are now internally assessed according to defined Criteria. Additionally, a new dimension – hypothesis formulation/problem solving and experimental design – has been added.

The detailed internal assessment of practical skills, and its contribution to the marks allocated to the total scheme of assessment, is long overdue. Nevertheless, it places additional stress on biology teachers who now have to attempt skills' assessment with large numbers of pupils, and in laboratories which may well be under-resourced.

This scheme is intended to minimise problems associated with assessment by providing the biology teacher with:

1. A comprehensive list of laboratory-based exercises from which teachers can select and incorporate into their teaching strategy. The 98 exercises incorporate 40 different skills, each of which is allocated to 1 of 7 skill areas.

2. Detailed coverage of the practical assessment of the skill areas *Hypothesis formulation/problem solving* and *Experimental design*.

3. Standard mark schemes, ensuring consistency of assessment (a) between teachers, and (b) whether a skill is assessed at the beginning or the end of the course.

4. A detailed section on materials and apparatus.

5. Specially designed copyright-waived worksheets which are easy to follow and incorporate many unique features to assist both pupil and teacher.

6. Information relating to many aspects of the internal assessment of practical skills and complete coverage of all Examining Groups' biology syllabuses.

Many of the experiments in the exercises are well known although, with each, I have attempted to introduce original material relevant to assessment. The *Experimental design* exercises, on the other hand, have a quite unique format which should be of benefit to both pupil and teacher.

Although the inheritance of ideas and experiments is, traditionally, the birthright of every science teacher, I would like to express my indebtedness to any colleagues whose original material has been the basis of my classes' experimental work since 1962.

David J. Newsham BSc
Head of Science West Leeds Girls High School

Contents

Chapter 1

The Format of Skill Assessment

INTRODUCTION

The scheme of assessment recognises 7 skill areas, each of which is subdivided into a number of discrete skills. Detailed mark schemes are provided for the 98 exercises which encompass over 250 skill assessments.

To maintain consistency of assessment, each skill is marked on a 9-point scale. The mark obtained by a candidate, for each skill assessed, is then assigned to one of three competency levels:

Competency Level III	9–7 marks
Competency Level II	6–4 marks
Competency Level I	3–1 marks

The format of each mark scheme is such that *all* candidates are provided with the opportunity to show what they know, understand and can do. However, a competency level of 0 is awarded in the extreme case of:

1. a candidate refusing to attempt an assessed skill;
2. the work attempted being worthy of no credit.

The relationship between the mark scheme competency levels, and the competency level requirements of each Examining Group's biology syllabus is detailed in Chapter 3.

ASSESSMENT OF THE SKILL AREAS

The scheme of assessment recognises 7 skill areas:

Following instructions
Manipulation
Measurement
Observation
Recording
Interpretation
Experimental design

Experimental design is a unique skill area at the 16+ level. The format of the *Experimental design* questions, and their corresponding mark schemes, is explained in detail in Chapter 2 (page 15).

All experimental work essentially involves two groups of skill areas:

Group 1 – process skill areas

These include the skills required to carry out successfully the necessary procedures in a practical exercise and are encompassed by the skill areas:

Following instructions*
Manipulation*
Measurement*

Group 2 – product skill areas

These include the skills required in order to record and analyse the outcome of the process skills and are encompassed by the skill areas:

Observation*
Recording
Interpretation

The formal assessment of the skills within a skill area designated with an asterisk * requires 'on the spot' evaluation by the teacher responsible for the supervision and authentication of experimental work. Where such assessment is required, the skill area on the mark scheme is also designated with an asterisk.

THE PROCESS SKILL AREAS

Following instructions*

The mark scheme for this skill area uses a rating scale which assigns candidates to different levels of competency depending on the amount of assistance required to carry out procedures safely, by following the 'stepped' instructions:

Criteria	Mark	Competency Level
Instructions followed *without assistance*. Procedures carried out *competently and safely*.	9–7	III
Instructions followed and procedures carried out with *occasional assistance*. Shows *awareness* of safety precautions but *sometimes careless*.	6–4	II
Instructions followed and procedures carried out only with *regular/ constant supervision*. Uses safety precautions *only when reminded*.	3–1	I
Incapable of following instructions and carrying out procedures, *or* skill *not attempted*.	0	0

For formal assessment of this skill area, the candidate must follow a minimum of 6 instructional 'steps'. Care has been taken that the instructions are clear and precise and the language used unambiguous. The candidate is also helped, in this respect, by the illustrations of equipment and, where necesssary, assembled apparatus (see page 31).

Manipulation*

Manipulative skills are those concerned with manual dexterity. The level of competency obtained by a candidate in this skill area is going to depend, to a large extent, on familiarity wth such skills prior to formal assessment.

Formative assessment, therefore, is going to have a direct bearing on competency level outcome.

Assessment criteria for the skill area *Manipulation* are used for the following skills:

1. Apparatus assembly.
2. Correct use of assembled apparatus.
3. The preparation of materials for subsequent investigation,
   using a variety of biological 'tools'.
4. Simple dissections.
5. Setting up a microscope.
6. Slide preparation of temporary mounts.

By the very nature of the skill areas, there is some overlap between *Following instructions* and *Manipulation*. In the latter case, competency is assessed using a number of discrete criteria. However, this is not intended to preclude teacher help in this area. For instance, the criteria for the assessment of the manipulative skill 'maintaining the temperature of a water bath', and the marks awarded, are:

Criteria	Mark
Bunsen remains alight throughout test	1
Low, blue flame maintained	1
Flame controlled using air-hole and gas tap	1
Sensible technique for cooling water if temperature rises above 40°C (e.g. add cold water)	1
Frequent temperature checks: with thermometer *in* the water; *but* raised off the base of the beaker	1 1 1
Temperature of water maintained between 35°C and 40°C throughout the test	2

Mark Obtained	0	1 2 3	4 5 6	7 8 9
Competency Level	0	I	II	III

The inability to take the water temperature in the manner prescribed would result in the loss of 1, 2 or 3 marks. Formative assessment could then be applied for one, or all, of these criteria and the candidate would still be able to gain 8, 7 or 6 marks for the formal assessment of this skill.

Where an exercise assesses both *Following instructions* and *Manipulation*, care has been taken to differentiate between each of the skill areas in the mark scheme.

Measurement*

The mark scheme assesses the ability to measure the following quantities:

Mass
Volume
Time
Length
Temperature
Area
Large numbers by systematic counting

Wherever possible, measurement of a particular quantity (e.g. mass) is included several times in the same exercise. This gives the teacher the opportunity, if required, to apply formative assessment when a candidate makes the initial measurement. Subsequent measurements can then be formally assessed.

The mark scheme criteria for the allocation of competency level III are as follows:

Quantity	Criteria
Mass	to within ± 1 g
Volume	to within ± 0.1 cm^3
Time	to within ± 1 s
Length	to within ± 0.1 cm
Temperature	to within ± 1°C

The criteria for the ability to measure area, and for systematic counting of large numbers, vary from one exercise to another and are dependent on the degree of difficulty of the measurement. Where a number of measurements of the same quantity are taken during an exercise, the competency level attained is awarded on the following basis:

All measurements taken satisfy the criterion	Competency Level III
All but *one* measurement taken satisfy the criterion	Competency Level II
All but *two* measurements taken satisfy the criterion	Competency Level I

Where only one measurement of a particular quantity is taken during an exercise, the competency level attained is awarded on the following basis:

Measurement taken satisfies the criterion	Competency Level III
Measurement taken does not satisfy the criterion	Competency Level 0

Throughout the GCSE course, therefore, recorded monitoring of each candidate's competency level in *Measurement* is going to be required so that the *highest* competency level for each measuring skill is entered on the Candidate's Record Sheet when it is finally submitted to the relevant Examining Group.

Although a low competency level attained by a candidate can be subsumed by a high competency level in *all* the skill areas associated with practical assessment in biology, the monitoring of measuring skills is going to pose the most problems. Because of this, the teacher needs to keep a running record, for each candidate, of competency level attainment for each quantity that is measured.

In isolated instances, some of the above criteria are too stringent in terms of the criteria required by a specific GCSE biology syllabus. So, as a precautionary step, the syllabus criteria must be checked and, if necessary, adjustment made to the above criteria.

THE PRODUCT SKILL AREAS

Observation*

The mark scheme assesses the ability to observe in the following situations:

1. Drawing of biological material obtained from dissection.
2. Drawing of biological material from observation using a microscope.
3. The grouping of biological material/organisms.
4. Comparing biological material before and after specific treatment.
5. Comparing and contrasting similar biological material/organisms.
6. The construction and use of keys.

All assessment which involves the drawing of biological material/organisms has basically the same format. Credit is awarded for drawings which satisfy the following criteria:

The drawings: are of adequate size;
are identifiable from the specimen;
have lines which are neat, clear and distinct;
have the scale stated;
include a feature, or features, unique to the specimen observed.

Assessment which involves comparison or grouping is either required in the form of a table, where features are described, or in the form of adjacent comparative drawings.

The assessment of the ability to *label* observed structures is confined to:

1. Using a text-book illustration to label unfamiliar observed structures;
2. Annotation of drawings where an important feature is not apparent from a pencil drawing alone (e.g. the *colour* of leaves of a plant which has been growing in the dark);
3. Annotation of drawings using prior knowledge (e.g. labelling of cell structures).

Assessment which involves the *construction* of keys uses a rating scale linked to the amount of teacher assistance required. Assessment of the *use* of keys awards credit for both the 'path' followed through the key and the correct naming of a particular specimen.

Recording

The mark scheme assesses the ability to record in terms of:

1. Entering results in a prepared table
The mark scheme gives:

(a) for the completion of a simple prepared table, a maximum competency level of II;
(b) for the completion of a more complicated prepared table, a maximum competency level of III.

2. Construction of a results table and the entry of results
This skill awards a maximum competency level of III. Results table construction will vary in terms of the data to be entered but, in general, credit is awarded for:

Heading data columns
Inclusion of units
Full set of results recorded
Identification of anomalous results
Results recorded in *single* table form
Clear overall layout

3. Construction of a graph
In constructing a graph, credit is awarded for:

Choosing a suitable scale
Labelling, with units, on both axes
Plotting points accurately
Joining points accurately
Writing a suitable title

Although the construction of a graph should, ideally, be taken from results obtained by an individual candidate during practical work, provision is made for candidates unable to obtain the necessary data by supplying a set of results so that this skill can be assessed without prejudice.

Interpretation

The mark scheme for the skill area *Interpretation* assesses the following skills:

1. Performing appropriate calculations on experimental data.
2. Extracting information from tables and graphs.
3. Suggesting methods of improving experimental techniques.
4. Applying theoretical knowledge to practical procedures.
5. Devising control experiments.
6. Appreciating the limitations of experimental procedure.
7. Applying experimental results to a wider field.
8. Recognising patterns.

Skill 1 is assessed using a rating scale which assigns candidates to different levels of competency depending upon the amount of assistance required.

Skills 2 to 8 are assessed by means of a series of structured questions. To assist the candidate to appreciate the weighting on each question, the mark is included in brackets.

There are two obvious problems associated with assessment of this skill area:

1. As a consequence of faulty practical technique, some candidates may have obtained no results, too few results or erroneous results. Patently, in such cases, meaningful interpretation of results is impossible. In such circumstances a candidate would be penalised twice for the failure to accomplish the practical skill(s).

   The mark scheme takes account of this. For exercises where interpretation of experimentally generated data is required, 'model' results are provided for candidates who fall into the above category. Such sets of results are provided where, traditionally, some candidates have problems associated with the skills required for the satisfactory completion of a practical exercise.

2. All too often, candidates obtain information relating to the outcome of an experiment from the questions asked at the end of the exercise. This, in itself, invalidates an investigative approach. The scheme of assessment is organised to obviate this problem.

   Questions associated with the interpretation of experimental results are set as a separate 'link' exercise (notated 'b'). In this way, candidates have no prior knowledge of either the questions or the outcome of the experiment.

   Thus the inclusion of sets of 'model' results, and the isolation of the skill area *Interpretation*, validates its assessment. This point is also referred to in Chapter 5 (see page 34).

Check lists for teacher use
Two copyright-waived check lists are provided for the recording of skills that require 'on the spot' assessment (see page 186).

Record of assessment sheet for candidate's use
This copyright-waived record sheet should be issued to each candidate at the start of the course (see page 190).

Chapter 2

Assessment of the
Skill Area
Experimental Design

INTRODUCTION

Teachers with knowledge and experience of 'A' level biology syllabuses will be well aware of the uniqueness of this skill area. Even with able sixth form students, the open-ended nature of experimental design questions places such candidates in situations where they are unsure, hesitant and lack confidence. At GCSE level, this problem is manifestly greater. The following notes in this section are intended to give guidelines to teachers in this most difficult area of internal assessment of practical skills.

The skill area *Experimental design*, encompasses the following 8 skills:

> *Identifying the problem*
> *Hypothesis formulation*
> *Selection of apparatus*
> *Experimental plan*
> *Experimental procedure*
> *Recording of results*
> *Interpretation and evaluation of results*
> *General evaluation of the experimental design*

Depending on the requirements of the syllabus being followed, some or all of the above skills are relevant to internal assessment. Teachers should refer to the appropriate section in Chapter 3 to ascertain which skills are required to be assessed by the Examining Group syllabus which their Centre is following.

EXPERIMENTAL DESIGN FORMAT

The exercises are rated, on the mark scheme *only*, according to difficulty:

Those titled *Experimental design 1* include:
> Apparatus selection
> Experimental plan
> (usually) Headed results table

Those titled *Experimental design 2* include:
> Apparatus selection
> Experimental plan
> Experimental procedure
> Recording of results
> (usually) Interpretation/Evaluation

Those entitled *Experimental design 3* include:
> All 8 skills

Enabling candidates to accomplish these skills is a daunting prospect. It is hoped that the following format, which applies to all *Experimental design* exercises, will ease the burden on both pupil and teacher.

Each *Experimental design* exercise is immediately preceded by a 'related' exercise involving a similar practical procedure which then must be slightly extended, refined or modified. It is thus *essential* for a pupil to have attempted the preceding 'related' exercise before going on to the *Experimental design* exercise. Thus, in order to attempt Exercise 5.9 'Which washing-up liquid', a pupil should have completed Exercise 5.8a and b 'Investigating the effect of bile salts on cooking oil' so that he has the relevant practical experience of comparing the appearance of cooking oil when subjected to different emulsifying agents. Similarly, Exercise 7.2 'Which salt solution?' could not be attempted without prior knowledge of Exercises 7.1a and b 'Investigating the effects of tap water and salt water on the mass of potato discs'.

This is not to say that all *Experimental design* exercises should be attempted *immediately* after the 'related' exercise, although this may be advisable in the early stages of the course to increase a pupil's confidence in this area. In the later stages of the course, *Experimental design* exercises could be set sometime after the 'related' exercise has been attempted. In this case it may be considered advisable to delete the number of the *Experimental design* exercise on the candidate's worksheet (e.g. remove 5.9 or 7.2) so that pupils are *not* given easy access to the method of procedure (i.e. checking back on the preceding exercise!)

Because the assessment of the skills encompassed by this skill area (with the exception of *Recording of results*) is achieved by using a 'rating scale' related to the amount of assistance given to an individual candidate, it is envisaged that a whole class of candidates could attempt a specific *Experimental design* exercise at the same time. Group work (2 or 3 pupils) is a particularly suitable vehicle in this respect, being advantageous to both candidates and teacher: candidates are encouraged to co-operate and discuss ideas, gaining confidence from each other, and the teacher has fewer areas to supervise and advise.

It must be stressed, however, that whereas *all* Examining Groups recognise group work as an available option in the assessment of skills, it is essential that a teacher is satisfied that an individual candidate working within a group is capable of performing that skill independently.

By setting *Experimental design* exercises at regular intervals throughout the course, the ultimate aim should be for each individual candidate to attain competency in the majority of skills in this skill area.

THE CANDIDATE'S WORKSHEET

The questions on the worksheet are structured in such a way that progression through each exercise follows a logical 'method sequence'. This is particularly important when attempting *Experimental design 3* exercises, where hypothesis formulation is required. In such exercises the candidates are:

1. Presented with the problem in simple language.
2. Asked to convert a key phrase in 1. into biological terms.
3. Asked to restate the problem in terms of a biologist.
4. Asked to formulate a hypothesis with reference to 3.

Once the hypothesis has been formulated, and the association with the 'related' exercise established, progression to the remainder of the skills can be attempted.

All syllabuses require the assessment of *Problem solving/Hypothesis formulation*, *Apparatus selection* and *Experimental plan*. Most syllabuses require, in addition, the assessment of *Experimental procedure, Recording of results, Interpretation and evaluation of results* and the *General evaluation of the experimental design*. Because of this, the candidate's worksheet is organised to accommodate all syllabus requirements:

> *Problem solving/Hypothesis formulation, Apparatus selection* and *Experimental plan* (including a blank results table) occupy the first two thirds of the worksheet.

> *Interpretation, Evaluation of results, General evaluation of the experimental design* occupy the last part of the worksheet.

Thus, depending on the syllabus followed, candidates should be provided with either the first two thirds *or* the complete worksheet (i.e. if necessary, blank out the last third of the worksheet when photocopying copies for the class).

THE TEACHER'S MARK SCHEME

The structured format of the candidate's worksheet is such that candidates should relate the problem, and its solution, to procedures adopted in the 'related' exercise. Each mark scheme is based on this assumption. However, teachers should not preclude the possibility of other viable alternatives being suggested by candidates.

Thus, if candidates suggest a feasible hypothesis, compatible with the problem, which differs markedly from the mark scheme format, there is every reason to encourage the development of this alternative experimental design. However, candidates 'branching out' in this way must be reminded of the exercise's 'frames of reference' – i.e. the experiment *must* be capable of being carried out in the laboratory, using readily available equipment, apparatus and materials, and the experiment *must* test the hypothesis.

Deliberately, the mark schemes for this skill area have been given a tight format – necessary in an area of study which can, very easily, be beleaguered by 'red herrings.'

THE SKILLS

Identifying the problem

The problem in an exercise is stated in simple terms and the candidate is asked to convert a key phrase into biological terms. Thus, in Exercise 5.13 'less fattening' converts to 'lower energy value (per mass)'.

Hypothesis formulation

Almost all candidates will need considerable help (at least initially) to achieve competency in this skill and, before formal assessment is attempted, it would be advisable to spend at least two single lessons (plus homework) discussing the basis on which a hypothesis is formulated.

Even after considerable discussion, a significant number of candidates could well be struggling. The mark scheme takes account of this and, if a candidate is still quite incapable of formulating a hypothesis, the hypothesis can be given and subsequent skills in the exercise can be assessed for the full competency range without prejudice.

In its simplest sense, a hypothesis is an educated guess that is capable of being tested. With reference to *Identifying a problem*, a hypothesis is a reasoned, single-factor answer to a problem, which is capable of being tested. For example:

Problem:
Why, on the same ivy plant, are the leaves growing in the shade smaller than the leaves growing in the light?

Valid hypotheses:
1. Light increases the rate of growth of ivy leaves.
2. The shaded leaves are in a more moist environment and this reduces their rate of growth.
3. The leaves in the light are subjected to higher temperatures than those in the shade and this increases their rate of growth.

A hypothesis would be invalid if two or more factors were proposed:

> Shaded leaves are in a moist, dark environment and these factors decrease the rate of growth.

Finally, full credit for this skill must be given if the hypothesis proposed by the candidate satisfies the following criteria:

1. It describes a single factor
2. It is testable (in terms of the exercise specification)
3. It is compatible with the evidence

This must apply even though the hypothesis may be highly unlikely.

Selection of apparatus

The *Experimental design* exercises use three separate methods for assessing this skill:

1. A selection of apparatus is made available, from which the candidate chooses the pieces that are required.
2. Essential apparatus and materials are provided and the candidate selects additional apparatus.
3. Apparatus is selected with no prior information.

In the case of method 3, apparatus selection should be based on the previous 'related' exercise. However, in most cases additional or modified pieces of equipment or apparatus are required and relevant credit should be given to candidates who appreciate this. Thus, in Exercise 6.6 'Which wavelength?', credit should be given for suggesting a device for holding the filter in front on the lamp. Similarly, in Exercise 5.8 'Which washing-up liquid?', a candidate *may* suggest a sophisticated piece of equipment to measure light transmission through the emulsions (i.e. a photometer).

Experimental plan

Having followed a staged plan in all previous exercises, candidates should appreciate the importance of writing out an experimental plan in a series of logical steps. They will particularly gain help from the 'related' exercise.

The experimental plan must:

1. Be clear.
2. Include all necessary apparatus and materials.
3. Specify amounts (e.g. 20 cm^3 water).
4. Be capable of providing an answer to the problem/test the hypothesis.

With reference to 4, it is common for candidates to design a workable experimental plan but one which is unrelated to the problem under investigation.

The following points are worth bearing in mind when discussing the plan with individual candidates or groups of candidates:

1. Neat, labelled sketches are useful, and in most cases superior to a written explanation of a set of apparatus.

2. If controlled conditions are required (e.g. constant temperature, light intensity, humidity, etc.) then these should be indicated.

3. If organisms are involved, and a control used, the organisms should be:

    (a) of the same stated number for experiment and control;
    (b) of the same species (i.e. all blowfly larvae or all woodlice if using a Choice Chamber).

4. If a factor such as temperature is being investigated, the temperature(s) should be specified.

5. A statement of *how* the factor is being 'measured' is required. This would be either:

    (a) the appearance of what is under investigation after a stated period of time (e.g. when the testa of a germinating broad bean seed splits; or number of organisms present in an area of a Choice Chamber); or

    (b) quantifiable measurements (temperature rise of water; mass of potato discs).

6. A statement of how *often* the factor is measured (minutes, hours, days) and for what duration is required.

7. It should be appreciated by candidates that replication of the experimental plan is desirable to eliminate any inconsistencies in obtaining just one set of results. (Time and resources will limit this only to *understanding the need* for replication.)

To guide a class of 25 or 30 candidates along the path outlined above is no easy task. However, the candidates will have the 'related' exercise to form the basis of their plan. Simple questions by the teacher, such as 'How will you make sure the temperature is constant?', 'What kind of seeds will you be using?', 'When will you decide when germination has taken place?', and 'How often are you going to measure the temperature?' will lead to the production of a workable plan.

The mark scheme rating scale will determine the competency level of the candidate, which will relate to how much assistance is required.

Experimental procedure

Most, but not all, Examining Group syllabuses require the candidates to put their experimental plans into operation and obtain results. In this case, the teacher has three alternatives:

1. As candidates will probably complete their experimental plans at different times, there is a case for having a staggered start – candidates, having completed their plan, move directly on to the *Experimental procedure*. However, there are a number of disadvantages to this, the main one being the inevitable interaction between candidates planning and candidates conducting the experiment. This problem may be due to the physical limitations of bench space or, more importantly to assessment, the gleaning of information involving, say, manipulative skill by candidates not yet embarked upon conducting the experiment. Also, a staggered start means that candidates are completing the procedure at different stages throughout the lesson – indeed some candidates may not finish the experiment by the end of the lesson.

    A point in favour of a staggered start is that, as candidates are at different stages, the individual assessment of the process skills can be made more readily, with fewer candidates to observe at any one time.

2. A complete double period can be devoted to assessing procedure, where all candidates have the same time to complete this skill.

3. Small numbers of candidates can be assessed in succeeding weeks, while the rest of the group are attempting problem-solving exercises using text-books or duplicated questions. This, however, would not obviate the main problem outlined in the first alternative.

Whichever alternative is adopted, the criteria which are relevant to this skill are:

Procedure followed competently.
Procedure followed safely.

Recording of results

In any experiment, results tables are produced in order that recordings can be seen and interpreted clearly. Possibly the best way of assessing a candidate's ability to record results is to determine whether or not the results can be understood by a second person who has not seen the experiment performed. The format for the assessment of *Recording* follows the same pattern as outlined on page 13.

Interpretation and evaluation of results

Interpretation of generated experimental results is a skill which this scheme regularly assesses, and candidates will be practised in the techniques of answering interpretation questions. Additionally, the format of the candidate's *Experimental design* worksheet is structured so that pupils are guided along the right lines.

Nevertheless, some candidates may need guidance in order to answer some of the *Interpretation* questions. This is acknowledged in the mark scheme

General evaluation of the experimental design

Essentially, this skill requires the candidate to be self-critical in terms of the experimental plan and procedure. Self-criticism is a particularly sensitive area for many adolescents, so any assessment in this area should be treated carefully by the teacher, particularly with candidates attaining low competency levels in the skills already assessed. Capable candidates generally have more self-confidence, are able to self-evaluate more objectively and are more ready to criticise their experimental design and suggest modifications and improvements. If required, this evaluation can extend into discussing possible areas of future study related to the experimental design.

Chapter 3

The Examining Groups' Syllabuses

.

This chapter is devoted to the relationship of this scheme of assessment with the schemes of assessment of each of the Examining Groups' syllabuses in terms of:

(a) Mark scheme criteria

(b) **i** General skill categories
     ii *Experimental design* skills

(c) General notes (where appropriate)

continued

LONDON AND EAST ANGLIAN GROUP

Mark scheme criteria

LEAG Skill Standards	Competency levels
High	III
Mid	II
Low	I

General skill categories

LEAG Skill Categories	Skill Area

Category A: Making and recording accurate observations
   i Drawing of biological material
   ii Comparisons of biological material
   iii Measurement with apparatus
	Observation
	
	Measurement

Category B: Performing experiments and interpreting the results
   i Procedure
     and use of apparatus
   ii Record of results
   iii Interpretation of results
	Following instructions
	Manipulation
	
	Recording
	
	Interpretation

Category C: Designing and evaluating an experiment
   i Plan of investigation
   ii Evaluation of experiment
	Experimental design

Experimental design skills

Category C: Designing and evaluating an experiment

LEAG Skills	Skills
i **Plan of investigation**	
Formulates a hypothesis/relationship with aims	*Identifying problem/ hypothesis formulation*
Appropriate methods chosen/techniques understood	
Validity of method	*Apparatus selection*
Proposed procedure	*Planning*
Worked procedure	*Procedure, Recording*
ii **Evaluation of experiment**	
Awareness of limitations of method	
Suggestions for methods of improvement	*Interpretation*
Suggestions for further work	*Evaluation*

Continued

MIDLAND EXAMINING GROUP

Mark scheme criteria

MEG Levels of Attainment	Competency Levels
High (9, 8, 7)	III (9, 8, 7)
Intermediate (6, 5, 4)	II (6, 5, 4)
Low (3, 2, 1)	I (3, 2, 1)

General skill categories

MEG Skills	Skill Area
1. Following instructions	*Following instructions*
2. Handling apparatus and materials	*Manipulation*
3. Observing and measuring	*Observation, Measurement*
4. Recording and communicating	*Recording*
5. Interpreting data	*Interpretation*
6. Experimental design/problem solving	*Experimental design*

Experimental design/problem solving

MEG Skills	Skill
(a) Identifying problem and planning investigation	*Identifying problem*
(b) Selecting techniques, apparatus, materials	*Apparatus selection* *Planning*
(c) Organising and conducting investigation systematically	*Procedure*
(d) Interpreting and evaluating observations and experimental data	*Interpretation*
(e) Evaluating methods and suggesting improvements	*Evaluation*

General notes

Hypothesis formulation is not required by the MEG syllabus.

NORTHERN EXAMINING ASSOCIATION

Mark scheme criteria

Competency level III equates with the criterion to be used in determining whether a candidate has attained the appropriate level of proficiency.

Lower competency levels do not fulfil the criteria for the 32 skills. However, competency levels I and II have importance in the *formative* stages of assessment and give a candidate positive information concerning the standard he has achieved. Moreover, the mark scheme will enable the teacher to indicate to the candidate, what *has* been done correctly and point out the areas which have precluded the attainment of the highest competency level.

General skill categories

NEA Skill Domains	Skill Areas
Measurement	*Measurement*
Observation	*Observation*
Handling materials and apparatus	*Manipulation*
Recording	*Recording*
Data and its interpretation	*Interpretation*
Experimental design	*Experimental design*

Domain: Experimental design

NEA Skills	Skills
6.1 Criticising experimental design including the use of controls	
(a) Identification of an uncontrolled variable. *Skill 27*	*Evaluation*
(b) Suggestion of an appropriate method of control. *Skill 28*	*Planning*
6.2 Formulating hypothesis	
(a) Formulating a hypothesis when the data involves a single factor varying in two distinct situations. *Skill 29*	*Identifying problem/ hypothesis formulation*
(b) Formulating several hypotheses in a novel and relatively complex situation involving factors which may interact. *Skill 30*	*Hypothesis formulation* (Exercise 8.10)
6.3 Devising an experiment to test a hypothesis	
(a) Specifying apparatus for the experiment. *Skill 31*	*Apparatus selection*
(b) Planning the sequence of the experiment. *Skill 32*	*Planning*

General notes

Following instructions is a skill area which is not assessed by the NEA Scheme for the Internal Assessment of Experimental Skills.

NORTHERN IRELAND SCHOOLS EXAMINATIONS COUNCIL
Mark scheme criteria

NISEC Competency Levels	Competency Levels
Top (3)	III
Intermediate (2)	II
Base (1)	I

General skill categories

NISEC Skill Areas	Skill Areas
Following instructions and carrying out procedures	*Following instructions*
Observing and measuring	*Observation, Measurement*
Manipulative skills	*Manipulation*
Recording/presenting information and Interpretation of results	*Recording Interpretation*
Experimental design/problem solving	*Experimental design*

Skill area: Experimental design/problem solving

NISEC Skills	Skills
A	*Identifying problem/Hypothesis formulation*
B	*Apparatus selection*
C	*Planning*
D	*Procedure*
E	*Recording*
F	*Interpretation*
G	*Evaluation*

SOUTHERN EXAMINING GROUP

Mark scheme criteria

SEG Skill Achievements	Competency Levels
3	III
2	I
1	I
0	0

General skill categories

SEG Skills	Skill Areas
1. To follow written and diagrammatic instructions	*Following instructions*
2. To handle apparatus and materials	*Manipulation*
3. To make and convey accurate observations	*Observation, measurement*
4. To record results in an orderly manner	*Recording*
5. To formulate a hypothesis 6. To design an experiment to test an hypothesis	*Experimental design*
7. To carry out safe working procedures	Safety aspects of the skill area *Following Instructions* as applied to practical work throughout the course

Hypothesis formulation and experimental design

SEG Skills	Skills
5. To formulate a hypothesis	*Identifying problem/hypothesis formulation*
6. To design an experiment to test a hypothesis	*Apparatus selection* *Planning*

General notes

1. An SEG syllabus requirement is that candidates must know of the 7 skills on which they will be assessed but *not* of the skills which are being assessed in each exercise. To conform to this requirement, it is necessary to delete (using liquid paper) the skill areas printed in the skill area table at the head of each candidate's worksheet.

2. Although the skill area *Interpretation* is not included in the SEG assessment of practical skills, teachers are strongly advised to incorporate *Interpretation* exercises into their non-assessed schemes of work (see Chapter 1, page 14).

WELSH JOINT EDUCATION COMMITTEE

Mark scheme criteria

WJEC Marks	Competency Levels
3	III
2	II
1	I

General skill categories

WJEC Skills	Skill Areas
1. Observational and Recording skills	*Observation* *Recording*
2. Measuring skills	*Measurement*
3. Procedural skills	*Following instructions*
4. Manipulatve skills	*Manipulation*
5. Formulation of an hypothesis and the designing and conducting of an experiment to test it	*Experimental design*

Experimental design skill

Category 5: Formulation of an hypothesis and the designing and conducting of an experiment to test it

WJEC Skills	Skills
Hypothesis formulation	*Problem solving/hypothesis formulation*
Design an experiment to test the hypothesis	*Apparatus selection, Planning*
Conduct an experiment to test the hypothesis	*Procedure, Recording*

General notes

1. The WJEC syllabus does not allow the assessment of more than 2 skills in any one piece of practical work.

2. Although the skill area *Interpretation* is not included in the WJEC assessment of practical skills, teachers are strongly advised to incorporate *Interpretation* exercises into their non-assessed schemes of work (see Chapter 1, page 14).

Chapter 4

The Candidate's Worksheet

Each candidate's worksheet incorporates a number of key features which have been specifically designed to aid both candidate and supervising teacher in the area of practical assessment:

1. The candidate's reference details
2. The 'Skill Area' table
3. The exercise notation
4. The sections of each exercise, titled:
   - (a) Information
   - (b) You have been given
   - (c) What you have to do
   - (d) 'Do not proceed further until your teacher has checked this Step'

The candidate's reference details

Name _____

Group _____

Teacher _____

Date _____

All Examining Group syllabuses require either (a) the submission of dated, documented evidence of a sample of a Centre's assessed practical work, or (b) the retention of all dated documented records and supporting assessed practical work at the Centre, for subsequent moderation. In both cases, the *original* work is required.

The candidate's reference details (top right of each worksheet) provides this necessary information and also serves as a check when marks are being collated to enter on the record sheets to be submitted to the Examining Group.

The inclusion of the teacher's name is important. Problems can become manifest in *any* scheme of internal assessment where a teacher either leaves the Centre, is absent for long periods or if a candidate is transferred to another centre. Where such a situation arises, the reference details give dated documented evidence of any such change that has taken place.

In the context of the candidate's reference details section of the worksheets, 'Group' refers to the *teaching* group/class/set, etc. to which the candidate belongs.

The 'skill area' table

Skill Area	Mark	Competency Level
Measurement		
Manipulaton		
Observation		

Each exercise (with the exception of Exercise 1.1) assesses at least one skill area, each of which is marked in accordance with the criteria supplied in the mark schemes for that exercise (Chapter 7).

For each exercise, the skill areas assessed are indicated in the 'Skill Area' table (bottom left of each worksheet) with spaces available for the teacher to enter the mark and competency level attained.

In addition, two blank 'Skill Area' boxes are included so that extra skill areas can be assessed if required (see page 33).

The exercise notation

Theme
This refers to one of the four Themes of the National Criteria for Biology.

Section
This refers to an area of the syllabus within a Theme (see 'List of Exercises' page 37).

Exercises
Each exercise is prefixed by two numbers. The first refers to the Exercise Section (of which there are 10) and the second refers to the Exercise Number of that section.

A number of exercises are 'linked'. These are notated 'a' and 'b'. For example:

Exercise 6.5a Investigating gas production by a plant during photosynthesis

Exercise 6.5b Interpreting the results of Exercise 6.5a

This is necessary to separate the skill area *Interpretation* from the practical work which generates the experimental results. This point is explained in Chapter 1 (see page 14).

The headings

'Information'
This is included so that the candidate is provided with a short summary of the exercise he is about to attempt and/or is given information concerning unfamiliar materials, apparatus and techniques required, or the way in which materials have been treated prior to practical work being undertaken.

'You have been given'

This gives a full list of apparatus and materials required. The drawings of apparatus and materials are an indispensable feature of the candidate's worksheet.

Drawings are used in preference to the traditional sectional diagrams for a number of reasons. Candidates, particularly the less able, can visualise equipment and apparatus construction more easily when studying such drawings. Moreover, if *Following instructions* and *Manipulation* are considered to be 'transferable skills' (i.e. skills which are of general use and not confined to the laboratory) then the precedence for 3-dimensional illustration has already been set: The assembly of 'flat-pack' furniture; the dismantling, cleaning and re-assembly of a central-heating boiler; the procedure for changing a car's fan belt are all illustrated in the manufacturers' handbooks by means of accurate, annotated, 3-dimensional drawings.

It is important to note, however, that the exclusive use of such drawings is *not* intended to preclude candidates producing sectional diagrams themselves. Familiarity with such diagrams is required not only in all science disciplines, but also for the end-of-course GCSE examination.

A useful exercise, in its own right, is the drawing of a sectional diagram of one of the many examples of assembled-apparatus drawings from the candidate's worksheets.

'What you have to do'

Each worksheet is set out in a series of short, simple steps giving concise details of experimental procedure. Where necessary, assembled apparatus is illustrated.

Candidates should be supplied with worksheets involving the skill areas *Following instructions*, *Manipulation*, *Measurement*, *Recording* and *Observation* 24 hours *at least* before the exercise is attempted. It is unrealistic to expect GCSE candidates to attempt a practical exercise without prior knowledge of the procedure, and they would be unduly penalised if presented with a series of instructions immediately prior to embarking on investigative practical work.

By having prior knowledge of procedure, the candidate is given time to assimilate what is required in relation to the apparatus, equipment and materials he will be using. Indeed, it could be considered that the reading of the worksheet and its assimilation is another example of a transferable skill.

Where the skill area *Interpretation* is being assessed (in terms of analysing generated experimental data), candidates should have *no* prior knowledge of the questions on the worksheets (see page 30).

By the same token, *Experimental design* exercises, if they are being formally assessed, should not be issued prior to the lesson.

'Do not proceed further until your teacher has checked this step'

This instruction is inserted on the completion of a skill which requires 'on the spot' assessment. Such skills (involving *Measurement*, *Manipulation* and *Observation*) require interaction between a single candidate and the teacher after a specific step in the exercise.

If chaos is not to reign during the assessment of these skill areas, some method *has* to be employed whereby each candidate can indicate that he has completed a skill which requires assessment.

If assessment of these skill areas is going to be effective, the number of candidates assessed per exercise must be limited. This is further discussed in Chapter 5 (see page 33).

Chapter 5

Assessment Strategies

FORMATIVE ASSESSMENT

In order for candidates of all abilities to do themselves justice in the internal assessment of practical skills, formative assessment is an indispensable aspect of pre-GCSE biology courses. Ideally, it should be incorporated into teaching syllabuses of the first year of secondary school education.

Formative assessment is by no means an innovative concept for any course which ultimately leads to a public examination. School examinations using questions from past 16+, CSE or GCE papers were, in effect, introducing candidates to the format and standard of questions that they were likely to encounter in the end-of-course external examinations. Subsequent 'post-mortems' of the questions attempted, including aspects of 'what examiners are looking for', are applying formative assessment.

The scheme of assessment which is used in the mark scheme of this book is a particularly suitable vehicle for use when formative assessment is applied in the laboratory. For each skill, the mark scheme format is consistent, throughout the 98 exercises, in terms of the criteria required. These criteria, used in formal assessment for GCSE, can be used as guidelines for formative assessment at the pre-GCSE stage. For example, early on in biology/science courses leading to GCSE, pupils should be made aware that, in drawing a specimen:

1. The drawing *must* look like the specimen and not like the drawing in the text book.
2. The drawing must be of a *reasonable size*.
3. A *sharp* pencil is required so that the lines drawn are clear and distinct.
4. The *scale* is required to give some indication of the actual size of the specimen.

Using the mark scheme criteria, *every* skill, and skill area can be used in this way to provide a scheme of formative assessment at the pre-GCSE stages of science/biology courses. Every pupil should be familiar with these criteria *before* embarking on the GCSE biology course. Moreover, if formative assessment is an integral part of pre-GCSE courses, the *formal* assessment stages in the fourth and fifth year become much less burdensome on the teacher because the candidates are *aware* of what is required of them for each assessed skill. In such circumstances, candidates are genuinely assessed on 'what they know, understand and can do'. Ideally, the ultimate aim of *formative* assessment is to place the *formal* assessment of practical skills in GCSE biology in true perspective – ancillary to the investigative practical exercises that are the basis of the study of any science discipline.

FORMAL ASSESSMENT OF THE SKILL AREAS

Following instructions, Measurement, Manipulation and Observation

For any one exercise, the number of skill areas that can be assessed and the number of candidates who can be assessed for each skill area will depend upon a number of interacting factors:

1. Examining Group syllabus requirements.
2. Class size and ability.
3. Availability of additional teacher support.
4. Availability of apparatus and equipment.
5. Prior formative assessment.

Because of the above factors it would be presumptive, to say the least, to lay down guidelines relating to how such formal assessment should be carried out. However, the candidate's worksheet, through modification, allows the teacher considerable flexibility in the assessment of the above skill areas and can be 'tailored' to suit the requirements of most teaching groups:

1. If an exercise involves the assessment of, say, three different skill areas and circumstances mean that the assessment of only one skill area can be accomplished, the following procedure should be adopted:

   (a) Make a single photocopy of the candidate's worksheet from the copyright-waived master worksheet.
   (b) On the copy, delete (with liquid paper) the skill areas not required.
   (c) Run off a class set of photocopies.

2. If candidates need to be assessed for, say, the skill area *Following instructions*, and this is not included on the worksheet for that exercise, then the following procedure should be adopted:

   (a) Check that the exercise has 6 or more procedural steps. If so:
   (b) Make a single photocopy of the candidate's worksheet from the copyright-waived Master Worksheet.
   (c) On the copy, add *Following instructions* on one of the blank boxes in the 'Skill Area' table.
   (d) Run off the required number of photocopies.
   (e) Assess this skill area using the standard *Following instructions* criteria (page 10).

3. If required, the instruction **'Do not proceed further until your teacher has checked this step'** need *only* apply to the few candidates who are being assessed for that skill area. This being the case, two forms of candidate's worksheets can be issued:

   (a) A few worksheets which include the '**Do not proceed . . .**' instructions for the candidates being assessed.
   (b) For the rest of the class, worksheets where the '**Do not proceed . . .**' instructions have been deleted.

By using this system, the number of *formal* teacher/candidate contacts is limited to the number of candidates being assessed for that particular skill area.

Recording

The skills within this skill area are:

> Entering results in a prepared table.
> Constructing a results table and entering results.
> Constructing a graph.

As long as the supervising teacher is satisfied that these skills have been attempted, unaided, it is possible to assess *all* candidates in a group at the same time. *Recording* skills can be assessed using the mark scheme criteria, after the practical session is completed.

Interpretation

The assessment of this skill area demands a different type of laboratory organisation. Here, a candidate is assessed on his ability to interpret the results he has generated from experimental work. In such a situation, it is therefore possible to assess *all* candidates in a group at one time with the proviso that the questions in *Interpretation* exercises are answered under supervised, controlled conditions.

As explained in Chapter 1 (see page 14), the format of the 'linked' (b) exercises enables *every* candidate to attempt such exercises. Alternatively, *Interpretation* exercises can be set for homework but then cannot be assessed formally.

WHEN TO ASSESS

For formal assessment to have validity, a candidate should be assessed only when he has reached a stage which represents a fair measure of his mastery of a particular skill.

Even in teaching groups which are set according to academic ability, there is invariably 'mixed' ability in terms of practical work. Because of this, some candidates in a group are going to take much longer to master a skill than others. Bearing in mind the limitations on the number of candidates who can be assessed formally for the skill areas *Following instructions*, *Measurement*, *Manipulation* and *Observation*, there are two possibilities:

1. Teacher judgement determines which candidates are assessed for a specific skill in each exercise.

2. Candidates' self-evaluation determines assessment. If formative assessment has been effective, candidates should be aware of whether they can prepare a temporary slide, weigh, draw, focus a microscope, etc. to comply with the mark scheme criteria. If a candidate is satisfied with the standard he has achieved in the formative stages of assessment, and the supervising teacher is satisfied that such self-evaluation is a true reflection of his skill ability, then discussion between teacher and candidate can result in the formal assessment of the skill in question. Such a decision should be made some days before the exercise (which includes the skill to be assessed) is attempted.

Self-evaluation

Self-evaluation has a number of advantages:

1. The candidate is not having assessment imposed on him.

2. Teacher–candidate interaction is enhanced. This is going to have important ramifications in the area of Pupil Profiles/Records of Achievement.

3. The candidate being assessed has demonstrated competency in the formative stages and thus the assessment process is positive rather than negative and confirmatory rather than diagnostic.

4. Because assessment is confirmatory, more candidates can be assessed at any one time for the same skill.

5. Using self-evaluation, the assessment of able candidates can take place earlier in the course, leaving the teacher free later on to concentrate on candidates who are struggling to master certain skills.

6. Self-evaluation in itself is a most important transferable skill.

CHECK LISTS

Copyright-waived check lists for use by teachers are provided in Appendix I (see page 186).

Each Examining Group provides its *own* record sheet(s) for the internal assessment of practical skills. These have been specifically designed to meet the requirements of individual biology syllabuses and are used when marks are finally submitted by the Centre in the Spring of the year in which the examination is taken.

However, in the assessment of skills which a candidate displays whilst working in the laboratory (skills that require 'on the spot' assessment) it is essential that a convenient clip-board check list is carried by the supervising teacher so that marks can be recorded, in accordance with the mark scheme criteria, at the time the skill is assessed. Such marks can then be totalled, for each skill, after the practical session is completed.

Check List 1

This should be used whenever the skill areas *Following instructions/Measurement/ Manipulation/Observation* are being assessed.

The vacant boxes, immediately below each skill area in the 'Skill Area' table (on the candidate's worksheet) can be completed according to the preference of the supervising teacher, e.g. for *Measurement* – the quantity being assessed; for *Manipulation* and *Observation* – a short-hand version of the sub-skills assessed and the part-marks allocated to each.

Check List 2

Where the skill area *Experimental design* is being assessed, a check list is needed to enable 'on the spot' competency levels to be recorded. This is especially the case when skills such as *Problem solving/Hypothesis formulation*, *Apparatus selection* and *Planning* are being assessed – the competency level may well be allocated on the basis of discussion between teacher and candidate. In such a situation it is important to record such competency level immediately after the discussion has taken place.

The four vacant skill boxes are for use by teachers who are following a syllabus which requires the assessment of one or more of the following:

> *Experimental procedure*
> *Recording of results*
> *Interpretation and evaluation of results*
> *General evaluation of the experimental design*

For each candidate, a tick in the relevant competency level column for each skill assessed is all that is required.

CANDIDATE'S RECORD OF ASSESSMENT

A copyright-waived Record of Assessment sheet for use by candidates is provided in Appendix II (see page 190). The skills applying to the Examining Group's syllabus which is being followed need to be typed into the relevant boxes before the sheet is duplicated (see Chapter 3).

At the outset of the course, each candidate should be supplied with a photocopy of the Record of Assessment sheet, to be kept in the loose-leaf folder/binder in which his completed exercises are to be retained. As each exercise is completed, the candidate should enter the necessary details on his personal Record of Assessment sheet. In this way, each candidate has his own documented record of competency level attainment.

Whether candidates should retain their practical folders and bring them to each lesson, or whether they should be kept safely in the department and issued when an assessed exercise is attempted, will be for the teacher to decide. However, as all syllabuses require that every candidate's personal record of practical work is available for inspection at the end of the course, retention of folders by the department would seem to be the sensible alternative. It is the author's experience that even the most conscientious candidate can 'lose' material required for internal assessment, almost invariably at the time when such assessed material is required by the Moderator!

CANDIDATES' PRACTICAL FOLDER LABELS

A page of printed labels is provided at the end of this book. These are for photocopying and attaching to each candidate's folder, providing a convenient method of standardising folder presentation in the department. This is particularly useful when the Moderator requires access to assessed material.

Chapter 6

The Exercises

EXERCISE LIST

Theme	Section
1. Classification/Diversity of Organisms	1. Classification/Diversity of Organisms
2. Relationships between Organisms and the Environment	2. Soil/Soil Improvement 3. Bacteriology
3. Organisation and Maintenance of the Individual	4. Cell structure 5. Nutrition and Digestion 6. Photosynthesis 7. Water Relations in Plants 8. Respiration/Blood and Circulation 9. Sensitivity and Response
4. Development of Organisms and the Continuity of Life	10. Plant Reproduction and Growth

THEME 1: Classification/Diversity of Organisms
SECTION 1: Classification/Diversity of Organisms

EXERCISE:

1.1   Constructing a key (1)

1.2   Constructing a key (2)

1.3   Investigating the gross structure of leaves

1.4   Leaf identification using a key

1.5   Twig identification using a key

1.6   Fruit identification using a key

THEME 2: Relationships between Organisms and the Environment
SECTION 2: Soil/Soil Improvement

EXERCISE:

2.1 Investigating the composition of different types of soil

2.2 Calculating the amount of water in a soil sample

2.3a Calculating the amount of humus in a soil sample

2.3b Interpreting the results of Exercise 2.2 and 2.3a

2.4 Collecting and observing nematode worms (round worms) from a soil sample

2.5 Technology – Investigating the effect of adding lime to a clay soil

2.6 Hydroponics – Germinating cress seeds to use in investigations into plant growth

2.7 The seed-size problem – *Experimental design 3*

2.8a Technology – Investigating the lack of certain chemical elements on the growth of cress plants

2.8b Interpreting the results of Exercise 2.8a

THEME 2: Relationships between Organisms and the Environment
SECTION 3: Bacteriology

EXERCISE:

3.1 Preparing a petri dish for growing bacteria

3.2 Infecting nutrient agar with a solution in which bacteria are suspected of being present

3.3 The growth of bacteria on nutrient agar

3.4 The milk-souring problem – *Experimental design 3*

3.5 Biotechnology – Designing an experiment to isolate and grow a specific bacterial colony from a petri dish of nutrient agar containing a number of different types of colony – *Experimental design 1*

THEME 3: Organisation and Maintenance of the Individual
SECTION 4: Cell Structure

EXERCISE:

4.1 Examining onion cells using a microscope

4.2 Examining rhubarb stalk epidermal cells using a microscope

4.3 Examining human cheek cells using a microscope

4.4 Examining the leaf cells of Canadian pond weed using a microscope

THEME 3: Organisation and Maintenance of the Individual
SECTION 5: Nutrition and Digestion

EXERCISE:

5.1 Testing food to see if the nutrients starch, protein and glucose are present

5.2 Investigating plaque on teeth

5.3a Investigating the digestion of egg white

5.3b Interpreting the results of Exercise 5.3a

5.4a Investigating the effect of amylase on starch

5.4b Interpreting the results of Exercise 5.4a

5.5 Finding the enzyme – *Experimental design 2*

5.6a Demonstrating a 'model gut'

5.6b Interpreting the results of Exercise 5.6a

5.7 Demonstrating digestion and absorption of a carbohydrate

5.8a Investigating the effect of bile salts on cooking oil

5.8b Interpreting the results of Exercise 5.8a

5.9 Technology – Which washing-up liquid? – *Experimental design 3*

5.10a Investigating the enzyme catalase

5.10b Interpreting the results of Exercise 5.10a

5.11a Comparing how much Vitamin C there is in different fruit juices – *Experimental design (1)*

5.11b Comparing how much Vitamin C there is in different fruit juices – *Experimental design (2)*

5.12 Investigating how much energy a peanut contains

5.13 The biscuit problem – *Experimental design 2*

5.14a Biotechnology – Investigating the action of a biological washing powder

5.14b Interpreting the results of Exercise 5.14a

THEME 3: Organisation and Maintenance of the Individual
SECTION 6: Photosynthesis

EXERCISE:

6.1 Testing a leaf for the presence of starch

6.2a Investigating whether chlorophyll is necessary for starch formation during photosynthesis

6.2b Interpreting the results of Exercise 6.2a

6.3 Investigating whether carbon dioxide is necessary for starch formation during photosynthesis

6.4   Investigating whether light is necessary for starch formation during photosynthesis

6.5a   Investigating gas production by a green plant during photosynthesis

6.5b   Interpreting the results of Exercise 6.5a

6.6   Which wavelength? – *Experimental design 2*

6.7   Extracting chlorophyll from leaves and separating the chlorophyll into its pigments

6.8   The leaf colour problem – *Experimental design 3*

6.9a   Investigating the action of potato juice on glucose

6.9b   Interpreting the results of Exercise 6.9a

THEME 3: Organisation and Maintenance of the Individual
SECTION 7: Water Relations in Plants

EXERCISE:

7.1a   Investigating the effects of tap water and salt water on the mass of potato discs

7.1b   Interpreting the results of Exercise 7.1a

7.2   Which salt solution? – *Experimental design 2*

7.3   Investigating the passage of water through the stem of a plant

7.4a   Investigating water uptake in the shoot of a plant

7.4b   Interpreting the results of Exercise 7.4a

7.5a   Investigating loss of water from the upper and lower surfaces of a privet leaf

7.5b   Interpreting the results of Exercise 7.5a

7.6   Investigating the distribution of stomata on the upper and lower surfaces of a privet leaf

7.7   Estimating the number of stomata on the lower surface of a privet leaf

7.8   Investigating rate of water loss (transpiration) from the leaves of a shoot

THEME 3: Organisation and Maintenance of the Individual
SECTION 8: Respiration/Blood and Circulation

EXERCISE:

8.1   Comparing the amount of carbon dioxide in inhaled and exhaled air

8.2a   Investigating gas exchange in other organisms

8.2b   Interpreting the results of Exercise 8.2a

8.3a   Biotechnology – investigating the effect of yeast on a sugar solution in the absence of oxygen

8.3b   Interpreting the results of Exercise 8.3a

8.4a   Biotechnology – Investigating the effect of yeast on dough

THEME 3: Organisation and Maintenance of the Individual
SECTION 9: Sensitivity and Response

EXERCISE:

THEME 4: Development of Organisms and the Continuity of Life
SECTION 10: Plant Reproduction and Growth

EXERCISE:

EXERCISE REQUIREMENTS (1): INFORMATION PROVIDED

Every exercise is included in this chapter and contains some, or all, of the following information:

Prior knowledge

In order that an exercise can be completed meaningfully, certain theoretical knowledge is usually necessary and information concerning knowledge of the syllabus background is included where required. By the same token, the need for candidates to know the function of relevant chemicals and reagents, and the reason for certain procedures, is also indicated. Prior knowledge is especially important if a candidate is to attempt successfully the skill area *Interpretation* (almost invariably set in the linked 'b' exercises) where questions relating to the previous exercise include relevant theoretical aspects associated with the practical work.

Advance preparation of materials

This section is primarily concerned with the preparation of solutions and materials prior to the exercise. It also contains information about 'household' materials that need to be acquired prior to the exercise being attempted.

Per station

Because of the possibility of candidates working in pairs, a set of apparatus and materials is allocated to a 'station' rather than a candidate. If the exercise involves 'on the spot' assessment of a skill, or skills, and both candidates at one station are being formally assessed, some additional apparatus would have to be provided per station. Thus, if preparation of a temporary slide is the manipulative skill being assessed, then two microscope slides, coverslips, scalpels, forceps, white tiles and pieces of biological material are required. A microscope and bench lamp would be shared – easing the pressure on expensive apparatus. An alternative is for all candidates to work in pairs *except* for those who are being formally assessed – again a saving on expensive apparatus.

Specific tips

This section includes helpful advice relating to each exercise. The tips include advice on:

1. Examining group syllabus requirements.
2. The source of materials not readily available.
3. The preparation of materials and solutions (if not included in the 'Advance Preparation of Materials' section).
4. The reasons for using specific materials/apparatus.
5. Prior treatment of materials.
6. The setting up of apparatus.
7. The need for a teacher to demonstrate a specific technique or manipulative skill.
8. The need for prior formative assessment.
9. Assessment techniques.

EXERCISE REQUIREMENTS (2): GENERAL INFORMATION

Capital equipment

The exercises have been devised to minimise the need for expensive materials and apparatus.

A class set of sheep's hearts (with attached blood vessels), for example, is not only expensive to buy but also difficult to obtain. The Scheme assumes that dissections involving such materials will be performed either as a teacher demonstration, or in groups of 3/4 candidates. In the latter case, formal assessment of an individual candidate's manipulative skill in dissection would not be possible.

In order to provide a comprehensive list of exercises from which teachers can select, and to provide coverage of the experiments suggested by the GCSE biology syllabuses, the following pieces of expensive equipment have *had* to be included for a number of exercises in this Scheme:

Electronic top-loading balance
This is required for Exercises 2.2, 2.3a, 2.7, 5.12, 5.13, 7.1, 7.2 and 7.4a. In these exercises, mass readings need to be taken to one decimal place.

Bench lamps
Microscopes which have no sub-stage illuminator incorporated require an external light-source. Direct reflection of sunlight via the microscope mirror into the eye is dangerous, therefore whenever an exercise involves the use of a microscope, a bench lamp is included in the list of apparatus.

Microscopes
One cannot escape the fact that a microscope is an invaluable piece of equipment of the GCSE biologist. Syllabuses, either by inference or statement, anticipate that candidates will use a microscope and be familiar with the adjustments necessary for the correct focusing and illumination of a slide.

The number of microscopes available to any one GCSE biology class must, sadly, be a matter of conjecture. Even if microscopes are available on the basis of one-between-two, the make, age, design and quality of one microscope may differ significantly from another used by a candidate in the same class. Whatever the situation, teachers are going to have to use their professional judgement when formally assessing the skill *Microscope adjustment*, even to the extent of slight mark scheme modification.

As with all skills, formative assessment has a large part to play in the assessment of the ability to adjust a microscope correctly. It would seem sensible that, if all types of microscopes available for use *are* of the same quality, a candidate should be familiar with the adjustment of one type only. Alternatively, if microscopes *vary* in quality, each candidate should be provided with the opportunity of being formally assessed using the most appropriate instrument available.

Microscopes are used in Exercises 2.4, 4.1, 4.2, 4.3, 4.4, 7.6, 7.7, 8.6, 8.7 and 10.4.

Stop watches/clocks
Although the use of a wall clock, with a sweep second hand, can be used in a number of exercises where only approximate timing is necessary, stop watches or clocks are required in all exercises where the measurement of time is an assessed skill.

Candidate's equipment

All exercises assume that each candidate possesses, and brings to the lesson:

Worksheet   Pencil
Ruler with cm and mm gradations   Pencil sharpener
Pen (working)   Rubber

Equipment/materials to be available

1. Despite the above assumption, it would be sensible to have available a few spare worksheets, rulers, pens, pencils, rubbers and a classroom pencil sharpener. This would ease the organisational problems at the outset of an assessed exercise. There is nothing more frustrating, at the start of a well-prepared practical session, than having a minority of candidates holding up the proceedings because of the lack of basic equipment!

2. A problem arises when the *Recording and Observation* skill areas are assessed on the basis of success in the *Following instructions* and *Manipulation* skill areas. For example, a candidate unable to assemble a piece of apparatus (*Manipulation*) would be unduly penalised if the subsequently assessed skill area involves using that apparatus to take readings (*Recording*). In such circumstances it is important that spare sets of assembled apparatus are available so that a fair assessment of the second skill area can be made.

3. For the *Experimental design* exercises, where *Procedure* is an assessed skill, class sets of apparatus and materials should be available. These will be, basically, those items used in the previous 'linked' exercise.

4. In exercises where scalpels are used, first-aid plasters should be available.

Materials to collect

To economise on apparatus, readily available 'household' materials are used wherever possible. Such items need to be collected and stored throughout the school year so that supplies are readily available when required. For example:

Used, clean polystyrene/plastic cups
Yoghurt pots
Plastic teaspoons
Margarine tubs
Freezer bag ties (with, and without, attached labels)

Most LEA schools' meal services supply yoghurt in 12-pack cartons. The indented, plastic bases of these cartons provide ideal trays for holding specimens or small reagent bottles.

Long-running experiments

It is inevitable, with biological investigations, that a number of experiments involve either:

    (a) Setting-up an experiment where recordings/observations/measurements are made the following lesson;

or (b) Setting-up an experiment which may run for a number of weeks, e.g. plant growth investigations.

Such exercises have been limited as much as possible in this Scheme because of the drain on apparatus, which becomes unavailable for use by other classes whilst the experiment is running. Moreover, 30 sets of apparatus take up valuable laboratory space and the chance of experiments being tampered with by other classes using the laboratory is a distinct possibility.

If an exercise *does* involve observations over or after a number of weeks, the apparatus used has been confined to relatively non-essential items of equipment – for example, used, clear petri dishes and plastic/polystyrene cups.

Whenever an extended investigation is required (i.e. completion of the exercise is not possible in the one practical session) then this is indicated on the candidate's worksheet and information is given as to when, and for what duration, observations are subsequently to be made.

SETTING UP THE STATIONS

Setting up 20 to 30 stations for an exercise is onerous and time-consuming for both teacher and technician. Additionally, the laboratory will almost invariably be in use immediately before the lesson in which the exercise is to be assessed.

One solution to this problem is to put the apparatus and materials required for the exercise on a side-bench in the laboratory some time before the lesson is due to start. At the onset of the assessed exercise, candidates select what is required to set up their own station, using the drawings on their worksheets for reference. At the end of the session, candidates return apparatus to the side-bench.

The skill area *Following instructions* could, justifiably, be extended to include the above procedures.

INDIVIDUAL EXERCISE REQUIREMENTS

SECTION 1: Classification/Diversity of Organisms

One of the problems associated with published material involving key construction and use is that observing *drawings* of organisms or structures can never really replace the observing and handling of the organisms or structures themselves. As such, the exercises in this Section which involve identification using a key, require the collection of fresh plant material (leaves, fruits, winter twigs) which are then lettered for subsequent identification.

In all cases throughout the Scheme, material which is relatively common and widespread throughout the UK has been carefully selected, although the *indiscriminate* collection of materials (particularly winter twigs) should be avoided at all costs.

Exercise 1.1 Constructing a key (1)

Prior knowledge: None.

Advance preparation of materials: None.

Per station: 1 petri dish, 1 dropping bottle, 1 boiling tube, 1 200 cm^3 measuring cylinder, 1 100 cm^3 beaker.

Specific tips: Centres following a syllabus that does not require the construction of keys can omit Exercises 1.1. and 1.2.

Exercise 1.2 Constructing a key (2)

Prior knowledge: Exercise 1.1.

Advance preparation of materials: None.

Per station: Scalpel, spatula, dissecting needle, inoculating loop, forceps.

Specific tips: See Exercise 1.1.

Exercise 1.3 Investigating the gross structure of leaves

Prior knowledge: None.

Advance preparation of materials: Holly tree leaves, 'grass' leaves.

Per station: 1 'grass' leaf (labelled A), 1 holly leaf (labelled B).

Exercise 1.4 Leaf identification using a key

Prior knowledge: Exercise 1.3.

Advance preparation of materials: Batch of the following leaves: ash, horse chestnut, oak, silver birch, sycamore, privet.

Per station: One lettered leaf of each of the following: A sycamore, B ash, C privet, D oak, E silver birch, F horse chestnut.

Specific tips: 1. Exercises 1.4, 1.5 and 1.6 can be used for key *construction* if the candidates are not supplied with the published key.
2. Help from the teacher may be required, initially, in defining the stages of identification.

Exercise 1.5 Twig identification using a key

Prior knowledge: Possibly Exercise 1.3.

Advance preparation of materials: Batches of the following twigs: silver birch, oak, ash, horse chestnut, sycamore, hawthorn.

Per station: One lettered twig of each of the following: A silverbirch, B oak, C horse chestnut, D hawthorn, E sycamore, F ash.

Specific tips: 1. Twigs can be placed in lettered boiling tubes.
2. The exercise can also be used as an introduction to the binomial system for the naming of species.
3. The collection of twigs, and the subsequent effect on the ecosystem, presents problems. Indiscriminate collection of specimens should be avoided.

Exercise 1.6 Fruit identification using a key

Prior knowledge: Possibly Exercise 1.3.

Advance preparation of materials: Batches of the following fruits: elderberry, hawthorn, rose, ash, oak, sycamore.

Per station: One lettered container with each of the following fruits: A elderberry, B oak, C hawthorn, D ash, E rose, F sycamore.

Specific tips: See points 2 and 3 of Exercise 1.5.

SECTION 2: Soil/Soil Improvement

Although the first six exercises in this Section stand in their own right, they have been essentially designed to link directly with relevant field work that candidates are undertaking.

Exercises 2.2 and 2.3 require the use of a balance which reads to 1 decimal place.

Exercise 2.6 should commence at the beginning of a term or half-term so that the development of the plants can be observed, on an uninterrupted basis, for 4 or 5 weeks.

If *Experimental design* Exercise 2.7 (The seed – size problem) is attempted, then this should also be started early in the term. During the course of growth of the French bean plants, Exercises 10.9 and 10.10 can also be attempted.

Exercise 2.1 Investigating the composition of different types of soil

Prior knowledge: None.

Advance preparation of materials: 2 soil samples – clay soil and sandy soil.

Per station:
(*1st lesson*):   2 soil samples 3 cm deep in boiling tubes labelled A and B, 2 bungs, boiling tube rack, 100 cm^3 measuring cylinder, 100 cm^3 beaker of water, 2 adhesive labels
(*2nd lesson*):   Boiling tubes A and B.

Specific tips: The constituents of each soil sample should be such that there is an observable difference between the layers that settle out in each case.

Exercise 2.2 Calculating the amount of water in a soil sample

Prior knowledge: Percentage calculations. Use of top-pan balance.

Advance preparation of materials: Fresh soil sample. Oven @ 100°C.

Per station:
(*1st lesson*):   One crucible, fresh soil sample (in 100 cm^3 beaker), chinagraph pencil, spatula.
(*2nd lesson*):   Crucible of dried soil.

Specific tips: 1. A crucible is used to obviate the problem of the transfer of dried soil to a heat-proof container in the next exercise (burning-off of humus).
2. A direct-reading balance which reads to 1 decimal place is required for both lessons.

Exercises 2.3a & b Calculating the amount of humus in a soil sample

Prior knowledge: Percentage calculations. Use of top-pan balance.

Advance preparation of materials: Dried soil samples from Exercise 2.2.

Per station: Crucible of dried soil (from Exercise 2.2), crucible lid, pipe-clay triangle, bunsen burner, tripod, tongs, heat-resistant mat, goggles.

Specific tips: 1. The need for *careful* testing of the hot crucible (Step 2) should be stressed.
2. A direct-reading balance which reads to 1 decimal place is required.

Exercise 2.4 Collecting and observing nematode worms (round worms) from a soil sample

Prior knowledge: Use of microscope and its adjustment. Folding of filter paper.

Advance preparation of materials: 5 cm length of thin-walled rubber tubing attached to filter funnels. Adjustable clips for tubing. Sample of loam soil.

Per station:
(1st lesson): Filter funnel with tubing attached, clip, coarse-grained filter paper, boiling tube, boiling tube rack, chinagraph pencil, 200 cm^3 beaker of water, plastic teaspoon, soil sample in 100 cm^3 beaker.
(2nd lesson): Assembled apparatus, microscope, bench lamp, petri dish base, chinagraph pencil.

Specific tips:
1. This method (Baermann funnel) has the advantage of not requiring the soil to be illuminated (unlike the Tullgren funnel method).
2. Whatman Grade 4 filter paper should be used. Paper (handkerchief) tissue is a good substitute.

Exercise 2.5 Technology – Investigating the effect of adding lime to a clay soil

Prior knowledge: Importance of soil porosity.

Advance preparation of materials: Dry, powdered clay. Limewater.

Per station: Two samples of clay (labelled A and B) 3 cm deep in boiling tubes, boiling tube rack, 40 cm^3 limewater in 100 cm^3 beaker, beaker of water, 100 cm^3 measuring cylinder, 2 bungs for boiling tubes.

Specific tips: Dry, powdered clay should be obtained from the Art & Craft Department. Red (terra cotta) is preferable to grey because flocculation is more easily observed.

Exercise 2.6 Hydroponics – Germinating cress seeds to use in investigations into plant growth

Prior knowledge: None.

Advance preparation of materials: Large number of used, clean plastic petri dishes; Perlite; cress seeds.

Per station: Petri dishes (see *Specific tips*), cress seeds in boiling tube, boiling tube rack, distilled water in 100 cm^3 beaker, 20 cm^3 measuring cylinder, 200 cm^3 beaker of Perlite, self-adhesive labels (1 per petri dish), plastic teaspoon, chinagraph pencil.

Specific tips:
1. Perlite is obtainable from Garden Centres. It is smaller grained and easier to handle than Vermiculite (which can also be used).
2. Examining Group syllabuses differ in the number of element-deficient investigations required. The number of petri dishes per station will thus depend on how many batches of cress seeds are being treated.
3. Germination is complete within 48 hours if the petri dishes (plus lids) are placed in an oven at 30°C.

Exercise 2.7 The seed-size problem – *Experimental design 3*

Prior knowledge: Possibly Exercise 2.6 in terms of setting up plant growth experiments.

Advance preparation of materials: For *Procedure* (i.e. available in the laboratory): batches of peas, broad beans or French beans; a direct-reading balance (if mass is used as the measurement of large and small seeds); growth medium; seed trays

Exercises 2.8a & b Technology – Investigating the lack of certain chemical elements on the growth of cress plants

Prior knowledge: Proteins contain the element Nitrogen. Function of proteins.

Advance preparation of materials: Petri dishes of cress plants (from Exercise 2.6); nutrient culture solutions.

Per station: Petri dishes of cress plants, test tube rack, test tubes (one for each batch of plants).

Specific tips: Plant Culture tablets can be obtained from the usual biological suppliers. Tablets are preferable to powder as the solution can then be prepared in small quantities (250 cm^3). This is ample for a class of 30. The solutions should be available in the laboratory (on the side-bench) labelled 'A Complete Culture', and 'B Distilled Water', etc.

SECTION 3: Bacteriology

Bacteriological studies are ideal for introducing candidates to the need for safety in the laboratory.

Teachers are advised to obtain copies of the ASE booklet *Safeguards in the School Laboratory* (*9th Edition 1988*) obtainable from: The Association for Science Education, College Lane, Hatfield, Herts AL10 9AA.

Exercise 3.1 Preparing a petri dish for growing bacteria

Prior knowledge: None.

Advance preparation of materials: Bottles of nutrient agar. Per bottle: 3 nutrient agar tablets plus distilled water. Allow to stand for 15 minutes. Loosen cap before autoclaving. Store in fridge. Prior to lesson, place in boiling water until agar liquefies, then cool to 45°C.

Per station: Bottle of liquid nutrient agar, sterile petri dish, bunsen burner, disinfectant, cotton wool, chinagraph pencil.

Specific tips: 1. A boiling tube with an aluminium-foil cover is an adequate substitute for a McCartney bottle.
2. Moving the petri dish before the agar has set (Steps 5 and 6) is a common error.

Exercise 3.2 Infecting nutrient agar with a solution in which bacteria are suspected of being present

Prior knowledge: Exercise 3.1.

Advance preparation of materials: Bacteria-infected liquid (see * below).

Per station: Petri dish and nutrient agar (from Exercise 3.1), bunsen burner, disinfectant, cotton wool, chinagraph pencil, bacteria-infected liquid, innoculating loop. Sticky tape and scissors should also be available in the laboratory.

Specific tips:
1. If Exercise 3.1 is omitted (i.e. pupils are provided with made-up agar plates), sterile technique *must* be explained.
*2. If Exercise 3.4 is going to be attempted, the bacteria-infected liquid should *not* be sour milk. Soil water is a useful medium and provides a link with the previous Section.

Exercise 3.3 The growth of bacteria on nutrient agar

Prior knowledge: Exercise 3.2.

Advance preparation of materials: Acetate sheet squares (9 cm). Black paper squares (9 cm).

Per station: Petri dish with infected nutrient agar (from Exercise 3.2), disinfectant, cotton wool, Acetate sheet square, black paper square.

Specific tips: It is imperative that candidates are warned of the dangers of removing the petri dish lid.

Exercise 3.4 The milk-souring problem – *Experimental design 3*

Prior knowledge: Exercises 3.2 and 3.3.

Advance preparation of materials: For *Procedure* (i.e. available in the laboratory): agar plates, bunsen burners, disinfectant, cotton wool, chinagraph pencils, innoculating loops, sticky tape, scissors, acetate squares, black paper squares, sour milk, fresh (refrigerated) milk, test tubes, test tube racks

Exercise 3.5 Biotechnology – Designing an experiment to isolate and grow a specific bacterial colony from a petri dish of nutrient agar containing a number of different types of colony – *Experimental design 1*

Prior knowledge: Exercises 3.1, 3.2 and 3.3

SECTION 4:   Cell Structure

Biological material used in this Section is easy to obtain and provides a good introduction to cell structure as a subject. However, the format of the worksheets and mark schemes can easily be adapted to produce other exercises involving, for instance, the investigation of unicellular organisms. Reference should be made to the section in the Teacher's Manual dealing with microscopes (see page 00).

Exercise 4.1   Examining onion cells using a microscope

Prior knowledge: Use of microscope and its adjustments. Cell structure.

Advance preparation of materials: Onions.

Per station: Microscope, slide, cover slip, bench lamp, white tile, scalpel, forceps, filter paper, iodine solution, piece of onion.

Specific tips: 1. The teacher should demonstrate how to break onion segments to obtain tissue.
2. At start of lesson, all microscopes should be 'wrongly adjusted' equally.
3. Because of the variety of microscopes the department might possess, Step 5 may have to be modified. Whatever the microscope, the criterion is a sharply focused, correctly illuminated slide, within the limitations of the instrument.
4. Step 7 assesses *Observation*. As such, and dependant on the eyepiece magnification, it may be necessary for the teacher to refocus on high power in order that this skill can be carried out. Any adjustment of this nature would, obviously, not penalise the pupil.

Exercise 4.2   Examining rhubarb stalk epidermal cells using a microscope

Prior knowledge: As for Exercise 4.1.

Advance preparation of materials: Rhubarb stalks.

Per station: As for Exercise 4.1. Replace the piece of onion with a 2 cm length of rhubarb stalk.

Specific tips: As for Exercise 4.1 tips 2, 3 and 4. The teacher should demonstrate the removal of rhubarb stalk epidermis.

Exercise 4.3   Examining human cheek cells using a microscope

Prior knowledge: As for Exercise 4.1.

Advance preparation of materials: Sterile cotton buds.

Per station: As for Exercise 4.1. Replace the piece of onion with a sterile cotton bud. No scalpel is required.

Specific tips: 1. With the increased awareness of diseases which are transferable by body fluids (e.g. AIDS), teachers need to check LEA guidelines before attempting this exercise.
2. As for Exercise 4.1 tips 2, 3 and 4. The removal of cheek cells and their transfer to the slide sometimes causes problems. It is important to stress that the area of the cotton bud which was in contact with the cheek, should be dabbed centrally on the slide.

Exercise 4.4 Examining the leaf cells of Canadian pond weed using a microscope

Prior knowledge: As for Exercise 4.1.

Advance preparation of materials: Sprigs of Canadian pond weed.

Per station: One leaf of Canadian pond weed, cavity slide, cover slip, forceps, filter paper, white tile, microscope, bench lamp, beaker of water, teat pipette.

Specific tips:
1. Because *Elodea* leaves have a curled lamina, cavity slides need to be used.
2. Focusing on specific cells provides something of a problem due to the superimposition of layers of cells.
3. As for Exercise 4.1 tips 2 and 3, high power is necessary for adequate observation of chloroplasts.

SECTION 5: Nutrition and Digestion

Although digestive enzymes feature prominently in this Section, it is important to stress the universal function of enzymes in metabolic processes. Exercise 5.10a investigates the activity of a non-digestive enzyme (catalase).

Exercises 5.12 and 5.13 require the use of a balance that reads to 1 decimal place.

Exercise 5.1 Testing food to see if the nutrients starch, protein and glucose are present

Prior knowledge: Food tests.

Advance preparation of materials: Food sample: mix 5% starch, 10% glucose, and 10% albumen.

Per station: Test tube rack, 3 clean test tubes, food sample in 10 cm^3 beaker, 10 cm^3 measuring cylinder, Biuret reagent, Iodine solution, Benedict's solution, bunsen burner, tripod, gauze, 200 cm^3 beaker of water, 100°C thermometer.

Specific tips: Albumen flakes are preferable to fresh egg white.

Exercise 5.2 Investigating plaque on teeth

Prior knowledge: Bacterial action on sugars in the mouth.

Advance preparation of materials: Pupils to bring from home: toothbrush, toothpaste, plastic cup. Spare clean toothbrushes should be available. Water carrier (2 litre) of clean tap water.

Per station: Ceplac tablet (½ will suffice), hand mirror, beaker.

Specific tips:
1. If this exercise is planned for a morning lesson, pupils should be asked not to clean their teeth after breakfast
2. Ceplac tablets are available from Colgate-Palmolive Ltd, 76 Oxford Street, London, W1A 1EN.

Exercises 5.3a & b Investigating the digestion of egg white

Prior knowledge: Properties of enzymes. Testing with Universal Indicator paper.

Advance preparation of materials: 1% albumen solution, 1% pepsin solution, 10% (2N) sodium
hydroxide solution, 10% (2N) hydrochloric acid.
A = hydrochloric acid/pepsin, B = sodium hydroxide,
C = hydrochloric acid, D = sodium hydroxide/pepsin.

Per station: 5 cm³ each of A, B, C and D in 4 labelled test tubes, test tube rack, 30 cm³ albumen
solution in 100 cm³ beaker, 10 cm³ measuring cylinder, bunsen burner, tripod,
gauze, 200 cm³ beaker of water, 110°C thermometer, Universal Indicator paper.

Specific tips: Albumen flakes are preferable to fresh egg white.

Exercises 5.4a & b Investigating the effect of amylase on starch

Prior knowledge: Food tests, properties of enzymes, a starch molecule = many linked glucose
molecules.

Advance preparation of materials: 2% starch solution, 1% amylase solution.

Per station: 10 cm³ amylase in test tube, 10 cm³ starch solution in test tube, 2 clean test tubes,
test tube rack, 10 cm³ measuring cylinder, spotting tile, iodine solution, 2 teat
pipettes, goggles, test tube holder, chinagraph pencil, bunsen burner, tripod,
gauze, 110°C thermometer, 200 cm³ beaker of water, stop clock/watch*.

Specific tips: *As accurate timing is not critical, a wall clock with sweep second-hand would be
an adequate alternative.

Exercise 5.5 Finding the enzyme – *Experimental design 2*

Prior knowledge: Exercise 5.4a essential.

Advance preparation of materials: 400 cm³ starch solution, 400 cm³ glucose solution, 400 ³
glucose and amylase solution. For procedure (available in
laboratory): apparatus used in Experiment 5.4a.

Per station: 3 test tubes labelled A, B and C containing solutions as given below.

Specific tips: Solution A = 5% starch solution
Solution B = 10% glucose solution
Solution C = 5% glucose solution and 5% amylase solution (ratio of 3:1).

Exercises 5.6a & b Demonstrating a 'model gut'

Prior knowledge: Structure of mammalian gut, villi, peristalsis.

Advance preparation of materials: 1% starch solution, 5% glucose solution and mix.

Per station: 50 cm^3 starch/glucose solution in 100 cm^3 beaker, 2 test tubes, boiling tube, test tube rack, 18 cm of 25 mm-diameter Visking tubing, iodine solution, Benedict's solution, 2 teat pipettes, spatula, paper clip, bunsen burner, tripod, gauze, 200 cm^3 beaker of water, 110°C thermometer, stop clock/watch*.

Specific tips: *1. A wall clock with a sweep second-hand is adequate.
2. The diameter of the Visking tubing is critical. This just fits into the boiling tube, and so water samples taken (Steps 8 and 9) are from a region close to the wall of the Visking tubing.
3. A demonstration of how to fill the Visking tubing is advisable:
   (a) Soak the tubing for a few seconds to make it pliable.
   (b) Knot one end.
   (c) Rub the sides of the tubing at the other end gently between thumb and forefinger.
   (d) Use the spatula to complete the opening.
   (e) fill the teat pipette and insert it into the full length of the Visking tubing. Discharge the contents.
   (f) repeat (e) until the tubing is three-quarters full.

Exercise 5.7 Demonstrating digestion and absorption of the carbohydrate

Prior knowledge: Exercises 5.6 a and b. Food tests. Properties of enzymes.

Advance preparation of materials: 1% starch solution, 1% amylase solution. Mix in ratio of 10:1.

Per station: As for Exercise 5.6a, except use 50 cm^3 starch/amylase solution in 100 cm^3 beaker.

Specific tips: As for Exercises 5.5a tips 1 and 2. Tip 3. should be omitted if an adequate demonstration was given in Exercise 5.5a.

Exercises 5.8a & b Investigating the effect of bile salts on cooking oil

Prior knowledge: Digestive enzymes. Bile stored in gall bladder, from where it passes to the gut.

Advance preparation of materials: For each station, 3 test tubes (with bungs) containing respectively 2 cm^3 cooking oil, 2 cm^3 5% bile salts solution, 2 cm^3 washing-up liquid.

Per station: Test tube rack, 3 test tubes (with bungs) containing respectively 2 cm^3 cooking oil, 5 cm^3 bile salts solution, 5 cm^3 washing up liquid, a 10 cm^3 measuring cylinder, ×8 hand lens, chinagraph pencil.

Specific tips: Prior practice in the use of a hand lens is necessary.

Exercise 5.9 Technology – Which washing-up liquid? – *Experimental design 3*

Prior knowledge: Exercises 5.8a and b essential.

Advance preparation of materials: For *Procedure* (i.e. available in the laboratory): test tubes, bungs, test tube racks, 10 cm^3 measuring cylinders, teat pipettes, cooking oil, 'Whizzo', 'Superclean' (×8 hand lenses)

Specific tips: 2 washing-up liquid bottles labelled 'Whizzo' and 'Superclean'.
'Whizzo' = proprietary brand.
'Superclean' = proprietary brand + methylated spirits in ratio of 4:1.
Test tubes must be clean and dry.

Exercises 5.10a & b Investigating the enzyme catalase

Prior knowledge: Properties of enzymes. Glowing-splint test for presence of oxygen.

Advance preparation of materials: Liver, potato, dried yeast.

Per station: Test tube rack, 1 test tube, 1 boiling tube, 80 cm^3 20 vol. hydrogen peroxide in 100 cm^3 beaker, white tile, 10 cm^3 measuring cylinder, 100 cm^3 beaker, bunsen burner, goggles, spatula, 3 splints, liver sample, yeast sample, potato sample, scalpel.

Specific tips: To relight the glowing splint, it is usually necessary to insert the glowing end *into* the froth itself (hence Step 6, instruction (b): '... as close as possible to the *surface* of the hydrogen peroxide.'

Exercise 5.11a Comparing how much Vitamin C there is in different fruit juices – *Experimental design (1)*

Prior knowledge: None.

Advance preparation of materials: None (apparatus selection is made from the drawings of apparatus on the candidate's worksheet).

Exercise 5.11b Comparing how much Vitamin C there is in different fruit juices – *Experimental design (2)*

Prior knowledge: Exercise 5.11a.

Advance preparation of materials: 0.1% DCPIP solution, fruit juices (see * below).

Per station: 2 test tube racks, 5 cm^3 of fruit juices A, B, C, D and E in lettered test tubes, 5 clean test tubes, 10 cm^3 measuring cylinder, teat pipette, DCPIP solution.

Specific tips: Proprietary brands of fruit juice are not very reliable. Use 'Shapes' lemon juice and dilute down to obtain the 5 'fruit juices'. (Undiluted, 5 drops of 'Shapes' decolourises 5 cm^3 of 0.1% DCPIP.) If this method is adopted, it is useful to have 2 of the 'fruit juices' with end-points close to each other. This will (a) discriminate well, and (b) introduce the concept of retesting.

Exercise 5.12   Investigating how much energy a peanut contains

Prior knowledge: Heat released by burning is a measure of the energy a food contains.

Advance preparation of materials: Untreated peanuts.

Per station: Stand, boss, clamp, 100 cm^3 measuring cylinder, boiling tube, 110°C thermometer, mounted needle, bunsen, peanut, water in 100 cm^3 beaker. (A direct-reading balance should be available for use in the laboratory.).

Specific tips: 1. The need to multiply by 4.2 (Calculation (a)) should be explained.
2. The mounted needles need to have sharp points.
3. A direct-reading (top-pan) balance is required which reads to 1 decimal place.

Exercise 5.13   The biscuit problem – *Experimental design 3*

Prior knowledge: Exercise 5.12 essential.

Advance preparation of materials: For *Procedure* (i.e. available in the laboratory): apparatus used in Exercise 5.12.

Specific tips: 'Ryvita Crackerbread' (or a similar product) is suitable. It (a) is dry and therefore heating in an oven to remove water is unnecessary, (b) remains fixed to a mounted needle throughout burning, (c) ignites easily, and (d) burns evenly and completely.

To afford a measurable comparison, the 'Slimmo' (or 'Dietex') biscuit need not necessarily be a slimming biscuit.

Exercises 5.14a & b   Biotechnology – Investigating the action of a biological washing powder

Prior knowledge: Properties of enzymes.

Advance preparation of materials: Packet of biological washing powder. Prepared 'soiled material.

Per station: Bunsen burner, tripod, gauze, 3 × 250 cm^3 beakers, thermometer (0°C–110°C), 200 cm^3 measuring cylinder, white tile, heat-resistant mat, forceps, spatula, plastic teaspoon, 4 pieces of identical oil-soaked material, 100 cm^3 beaker containing biological washing powder..

Specific tips: Soak pieces of material (white cotton, 3 cm × 3 cm) in 'coloured' oil (e.g. linseed).

THE EXERCISES

SECTION 6:   Photosynthesis

The availability of adequate supplies of suitable plant material is a priority for this section. Stem-cutting propagation of geranium plants (including the variegated variety) should be started at the beginning of the Autumn term if this Section is to be attempted in the following Summer term. Large, overgrown plants can be obtained quite cheaply at Garden Centres in September/October and used for taking cuttings. If sunlight, as opposed to artificial light, is the source of illumination for investigations which test leaves for the presence of starch, results obtained are very much influenced by weather conditions. If possible, these exercises should be attempted in lessons which commence during mid-morning or afternoon sessions, when better results can be expected.

Exercise 6.1   Testing a leaf for the presence of starch

Prior knowledge: If this and subsequent exercises in Section 6 are investigatory, no prior knowledge is required. If the exercises are confirmatory, an outline knowledge of photosynthesis is required.

Advance preparation of materials: Soft-leaved pot plants (e.g. geranium, tradescantia) previously exposed to light prior to the exercise.

Per station: Bunsen burner, tripod, gauze, forceps, beaker of water, white tile, iodine solution, petri dish base, 1 leaf.

Specific tips: 1. The teacher should supply the boiling tube and ethanol, as and when each station reaches Step 3.
2. For Exercise 6.1, the decolourising of the leaf and treatment with iodine solution is assessed for the skill area *Following instructions*. This is to allow pupils to familiarise themselves with the stages. In subsequent exercises in Section 6, this procedure is assessed for the skill area *Manipulation*.

Exercises 6.2a & b   Investigating whether chlorophyll is necessary for starch formation during photosynthesis

Prior knowledge: Exercise 6.1.

Advance preparation of materials: Soft-leaved *variegated* pot plants previously exposed to light prior to this exercise.

Per station: As for Exercise 6.1, except a variegated leaf should be used.

Specific tips: See 1 and 2 of Exercise 6.1.

Exercise 6.3 Investigating whether carbon dioxide is necessary for starch formation during photosynthesis

Prior knowledge: Exercise 6.1. Sodium hydroxide as a carbon dioxide absorbent. Sodium hydrogen carbonate as a substance which increases carbon dioxide concentration.

Advance preparation of materials: Two destarched, leafy, potted geranium plants. Container of sodium hydroxide in one pot, container of saturated sodium carbonate solution in another pot. Both pots enclosed in transparent polythene bags and placed in light for 48 hours.

Per station: Bunsen burner, tripod, gauze, forceps, beaker of water, white tile, iodine solution, 2 petri dish bases, 1 freezer bag tie.

Specific tips: See tips 1 and 2 of Exercise 6.1.

Exercise 6.4 Investigating whether light is necessary for starch formation during photosynthesis

Prior knowledge: Exercise 6.1.

Advance preparation of materials: Destarched potted plants under light-proof covers.

Per station:
(1st lesson): A piece of aluminium (cooking) foil (10 cm × 10 cm), scissors, 2 paper clips.
(2nd lesson): Bunsen burner, tripod, gauze, forceps, beaker of water, white tile, iodine solution.

Specific tips: See tips 1. and 2. of Exercise 6.1. One plant per bench. Large empty catering tins of chopped tomatoes, etc. are good light-proof containers. (These are obtainable from restaurant kitchens.)

Exercises 6.5a & b Investigating gas production by a green plant during photosynthesis

Prior knowledge: Oxygen is evolved during photosynthesis. Test for oxygen.

Advance preparation of materials: Sprigs of Canadian pond weed.

Per station: 250 cm^3 beaker of water, 100 cm^3 measuring cylinder, white tile, scalpel, stop clock/watch, $\frac{1}{2}$ metre rule, bench lamp, freezer-bag tie, 100 cm^3 beaker containing sodium hydrogen carbonate crystals.

Specific tips:
1. The laboratory needs to be darkened.
2. Pond weed should be well illuminated prior to lesson.
3. Scalpels must be sharp to ensure a clean cut.
4. Paper clips (the usual method of 'weighting' the pond weed) tend to be too light.
5. The collection of the oxygen evolved, and its subsequent testing with a glowing splint, should be done as a demonstration after completion of Exercise 6.5b. Large numbers of sprigs of pond weed are required to obtain a suitable volume of gas.

Exercise 6.6 Which wavelength? – *Experimental design 2*

Prior knowledge: Exercises 6.5a and b.

Advance preparation of materials: For *Procedure* (i.e. available in the laboratory): apparatus and materials as for Exercises 6.5a. Stands, bosses, clamps, gel filters.

Specific tips: Gel filters can be obtained from: Donmar Sales, Shorts Gardens, London WC2 (Tel. 01-836 1801).
Further information on gel filters is available from: Association of British Theatre Technicians (ABTT), 4 Great Putney St., London W1R 3DF (Tel. 01-434 3901).

Exercise 6.7 Extracting chlorophyll from leaves and separating the chlorophyll into its pigments

Prior knowledge: Use of pestle and mortar. Filtration.

Advance preparation of materials: Large 'soft' leaves (e.g. dead-nettle) boiled for 2 minutes. Solvent – petroleum ether (40°–60° boiling point) and acetone, ratio 9:1. Pieces of chromatography paper (15 cm × 1.5 cm).

Per station: 6 boiled leaves, scissors, scalpel, forceps, white tile, pestle and mortar, boiling tube rack, boiling tube and cork, filter funnel, filter paper, 100 cm^3 beaker, chromatography paper, pin, drawing pin, paper towel.

Specific tips: Chlorophyll extract should be available in case some pupils are unable to obtain a satisfactory volume of filtrate (i.e. so the skill area *Observation* can be assessed). This extract should be kept in the dark.

Exercise 6.8 The leaf colour problem - *Experimental design 3*

Prior knowledge: Exercise 6.7.

Advance preparation of materials: For *Procedure* (i.e. available in the laboratory): apparatus and materials as for Exercise 6.7. Substitute copper beech leaves for dead nettle leaves

Specific tips: 1. Any 'non-green' leaves will suffice. If leaves other than copper beech are used, the plant name should be altered in the section titled 'Information' on the candidate's worksheet.
2. The pre-treatment of the leaves (i.e. boiling) should not be done in the laboratory; batches of leaves should be boiled prior to the assessment of the skill *Procedure*.

Exercises 6.9a & b Investigating the action of potato juice on glucose

Prior knowledge: Use of pestle and mortar. Filtration. Starch test.

Advance preparation of materials: 5% glucose-1-phosphate solution. Potatoes – peeled, cubed (approx 1 cm^3) and kept under water.

Per station: Two cubes of potato, 10 cm^3 measuring cylinder, spatula, pestle and mortar, filter funnel, filter paper, spotting tile, teat pipette, iodine solution, test tube rack, clean test tube, test tube of glucose-1-phosphate, stop watch/clock, sand.

Specific tips: 1. Potato juice extract (previously tested to check for the absence of starch) should be available. It is important that all pupils have a starch-free extract.
2. Glucose-1-phosphate is expensive. 1 cm^3 is adequate for each station. An alternative is for each pupil to obtain ⅓rd of a pipette full from the teacher.

SECTION 7: Water Relations in Plants

Exercises 7.1, 7.2 and 7.4 require the use of a balance which reads to 1 decimal place.

Exercises 7.1a & b Investigating the effects of tap water and salt water on the mass of potato discs

Prior knowledge: Osmosis. Plasmolysis. Use of the laboratory balance.

Advance preparation of materials: Using large 'old' potatoes, peel and cut into cylinders with a 2 cm diameter cork-borer prior to the lesson. Place in a large (1 litre) beaker of tap water until ready for immediate use.

Per station: White tile, scalpel, section lifter, 6 filter papers, 50 cm^3 salt water in a 100 cm^3 beaker, 50 cm^3 tape water in a 100 cm^3 beaker (both beakers labelled), potato cylinders. A direct-reading balance, should be available for use in the laboratory.

Specific tips: 1. A direct-reading (top-pan) balance which reads to 1 decimal place is required.
2. Use 20% salt solution.
3. Per station, provide enough potato cylinders for 20 discs.

Exercise 7.2 Which salt solution? – *Experimental design 2*

Prior knowledge: Exercise 7.1 essential.

Advance preparation of materials: For *Procedure* (i.e. available in the laboratory): apparatus and equipment as for Exercise 7.1.
A = 10% solution ⎫ for a class of 30 pupils, approximately
B = 20% solution ⎬ 2 litres of each solution is required
C = 1% solution ⎭

Exercise 7.3 Investigating the passage of water through the stem of a plant

Prior knowledge: None.

Advance preparation of materials: Celery stalks in red dye for 24 hours.

Per station: Bench lamp, microscope, 2 microscope slides, white tile, scalpel, forceps, mounted needle, 3 cm length of red-stained celery stalk.

Specific tips: 1. Water can be coloured by red ink/Eosin/any red vegetable dye.
2. All microscopes should be 'wrongly adjusted' equally.
Tips 3. and 4. as for Exercise 4.1.
It is helpful if some stalks of celery are left in the beaker of dye and displayed on the front bench.

Exercises 7.4a & b Investigating water uptake in the shoot of a plant

Prior knowledge: Water and turgidity of cells. Water required in cell metabolism. Energy production results in loss of mass. Use of balance.

Advance preparation of materials: Leafy shoots (1 per station) in water.

Per station: 20 cm^3 measuring cylinder, 2 cm^3 oil in a test tube, test tube rack, 1 adhesive label, leafy shoot in a beaker of water.

Specific tips: Use soft tissue shoots (e.g. dead-nettle) with as big a leaf area as possible. A direct reading (top-pan) balance which reads to 1 decimal place is required.

Exercises 7.5a & b Investigating loss of water from the upper and lower surfaces of a privet leaf

Prior knowledge: Cobalt chloride paper as a moisture detector.

Advance preparation of materials: Cobalt chloride paper in desiccator. Large privet leaves.

Per station: Bunsen burner, forceps, white tile, stop clock/watch, piece of cobalt chloride paper, privet leaf, pair of scissors, 5 cm length of sticky tape.

Specific tips: Keep the cobalt chloride paper in the desiccator until ready for use.

Exercise 7.6 Investigating the distribution of stomata on the upper and lower surfaces of a privet leaf

Prior knowledge: Stomata. Guard cells.

Advance preparation of materials: Privet leaves, clear nair varnish.

Per station: Bench lamp, microscope, microscope slide, 2 cover slips, chinagraph pencil, scalpel, forceps, teat pipette, clear nail varnish, filter paper, beaker of water, privet leaf, white tile.

Specific tips: See tips 2, 3 and 4 of Exercise 4.1.

Exercise 7.7 Estimating the number of stomata on the lower surface of a privet leaf

Prior knowledge: Stomata. Guard cells.

Advance preparation of materials: Privet leaves (see Mark Scheme), clear nair varnish.

Per station: Bench lamp, microscope, microscope slide, cover slip, scalpel, forceps, beaker of water, teat pipette, privet leaf, clear nail varnish, white tile.

Specific tips: See Mark Scheme for (a) leaf selection, and (b) checking area of leaf. Stomatal counts, without a graticule, are difficult - hence the generous error-allowance in the Mark Scheme.
See also tips 2, 3 and 4 of Exercise 4.1.

Exercise 7.8 Investigating rate of water loss (transpiration) from the leaves of a shoot

Prior knowledge: Transpiration.

Advance preparation of materials: Leafy shoots, capillary tubing (12 cm lengths).

Per station: Lamp, stand, boss, clamp, 3 cm rubber tubing, chinagraph pencil, filter paper, stop clock/watch, leafy shoot in beaker of water, capillary tubing.

Specific tips: This is a very difficult piece of apparatus to set up.
1. Each station needs access to a sink or deep bowl.
2. The cross-section of the cut end of the shoot must be circular and fit tightly into the rubber tubing. Young woody shoots (e.g. sycamore and horse chestnut) tend to produce the best results.
3. Petroleum jelly should be available, but not used unless it is necessary. Invariably, the jelly is accidentally transferred to the leaf surfaces.

SECTION 8: Respiration/Blood and Circulation

Exercises 8.2 to 8.5 require a basic knowledge of cell respiration. Exercises 8.7 and 8.8, which both require the taking of blood samples, need careful consideration. Future DES/LEA instructions to schools and colleges could well prohibit this procedure. The DES has produced an advice booklet which has been sent to all schools – *Children at school and problems related to AIDS* (*March 1986*). It recommends 'no HTLV-III/LAV antibody positive person should give blood for class use'.

Even in the unlikely event of no further directives, it would appear essential that a consent form should be signed by the candidate's parent/guardian giving permission for a blood sample to be taken. Additionally, teachers are advised to obtain copies of the ASE booklet *Safeguards in the School Laboratory* (*ninth edition, 1988*) obtainable from:

The Association for Science Education
College Lane,
Hatfield,
Herts.,
AL10 9AA.

Exercise 8.1 Comparing the amount of carbon dioxide in inhaled and exhaled air

Prior knowledge: Limewater test for carbon dioxide.

Advance preparation of materials: Right-angled glass tubing. Limewater.

Per station: 2 boiling tubes, boiling tube rack, 2 (2-holed) rubber bungs, 2 pieces of rubber tubing to fit over glass tubing, 4 pieces of right-angled glass tubing, glass T-piece, beaker of limewater, beaker of water.

Specific tips: 1. Ensure the ends of the glass tubing are 'flamed' to remove any sharp edges.
2. Ensure the glass tubing will fit easily through the holes in the rubber bung (i.e. force should not be required).

Exercises 8.2a & b Investigating gas exchange in other organisms

Prior knowledge: Basics of cell respiration. Carbon dioxide is absorbed by sodium hydroxide.

Advance preparation of materials: Germinating peas (soaked for 48 hours), blowfly larvae, right-angled capillary tubing.

Per station: Boiling tube rack, 2 boiling tubes each containing 2 cm^3 of sodium hydroxide solution, 3 100 cm^3 beakers containing approximately 15 germinating peas, 15 poppet beads and 30 blowfly larvae, 2 pieces of right-angled capillary tubing, 2 (1-holed) rubber bungs, 2 wire 'cages', small beaker of red ink, teat pipette, pair of blunt forceps.

Specific tips: This is a very difficult experiment for obtaining consistent results (even using a water bath).
1. To obtain satisfactory results, ensure that the maximum number of respiring organisms is placed in the respirometer.
2. To make a wire 'cage', cut sheets of perforated zinc into strips of 9 cm × 2 cm. Bend into a 'U' shape. (NB. Perforated zinc sheets 12″ × 12″ are available from most DIY shops.)

Exercises 8.3a & b Biotechnology – Investigating the effect of yeast on a sugar solution in the absence of oxygen

Prior knowledge: Actively respiring organisms produce heat.

Advance preparation of materials: Boiled and cooled sugar solution. Yeast suspension, glass, J-tubing.

Per station:
(1st lesson):   Boiling tube rack, boiling tube, 1 (1-holed) bung/cork, boiling tube of boiled and cooled sugar solution, test tube containing 2 cm^3 oil, test tube containing 25 cm^3 yeast suspension, clean test tube, piece of glass J-tubing, 50 cm^3 measuring cylinder, chinagraph pencil.

(2nd lesson):   Assembled apparatus, 110°C thermometer.

Specific tips: 1. Hydrogen carbonate indicator solution should be kept in an aspirator immediately prior to use (hence Step 5).
2. The J-tubing should be bent so that it will allow the apparatus (boiling tube and test tube) to stand in a boiling tube rack.

Exercises 8.4a & b Biotechnology – Investigating the effect of yeast on dough

Prior knowledge: Respiring organisms produce carbon dioxide.

Advance preparation of materials: Activation of yeast, empty margarine tubs, polystyrene coffee cups*, plastic teaspoons.

Per station: 2 clean beakers (200 cm^3), 100 cm^3 beaker containing 2 teaspoons of sugar, 200 cm^3 beaker containing 10 teaspoons of plain flour, 100 cm^3 beaker of water, test tube rack, test tube of oil, test tube containing 2 cm^3 activated yeast, 20 cm^3 measuring cylinder, chinagraph pencil, filter paper, plastic container (margarine tub), plastic teaspoon, spatula, paper towel.

Specific tips: To save on beakers, all containers can be disposable, e.g. polystyrene/plastic coffee cups*. The problem, however, with using opaque containers is that the presence of carbon dioxide bubbles in the dough and yeast is not detectable.

Exercise 8.5 Biotechnology – The ideal loaf – *Experimental design 3*

Prior knowledge: Exercises 8.3 and 8.4.

Advance preparation of materials: For *Procedure* (i.e. available in laboratory): activated yeast, test tubes, test tube racks, bunsen burners, tripods, gauzes, 200 cm^3 beakers, 0–110°C thermometers, 10 cm^3 measuring cylinders.

Exercise 8.6 Investigating (a) the external features of a fish, and (b) gill structure

Prior knowledge: Lung structure.

Advance preparation of materials: Whitebait.

Per station: Bench lamp, microscope, microscope slide, white tile, pair of forceps, pair of pointed dissecting scissors, beaker of water, teat pipette, whitebait.

Specific tips: 1. Sprats are an alternative. Whitebait are in season May–August, sprats are in season October–March. Both fish can be obtained from wholesale fish merchants. Purchased fish often have damaged caudal fins.
2. Soap is required for washing hands after the dissection is completed.

Exercise 8.7 Observing blood cells

Prior knowledge: None.

Advance preparation of materials: Leishmann's stain, 10% glycerine.

Per station: Microscope, bench lamp, 2 microscope slides, 1 cover slip, white tile, 100 cm^3 beaker, 2 pieces of filter paper, sterile lancet (1 per pupil), boiling tube rack, boiling tube of antiseptic, cotton wool, 10% glycerine, Leishmann's stain.

Specific tips: 1. See Introduction to Section 8 (page 000).
2. Propan-2-ol (isopropyl alcohol) is a suitable antiseptic.

Exercise 8.8 Determining blood groups

Prior knowledge: None.

Advance preparation of materials: None.

Per station: Microscope slide, sterile lancet (1 per pupil), boiling tube rack, boiling tube of antiseptic, white tile, spatula, chinagraph pencil, 100 cm^3 beaker, cotton wool, 2 pieces of filter paper.

Specific tips: 1. See Introduction to Section 8 (page 000).
2. Sera should be stored in a refrigerator until used.
3. Blood grouping sera can be obtained from: A. R. Horwell (Reagents) Ltd, 73 Maygrove Road, West Hampstead, London, NW6 2BP.

Exercises 8.9a & b Investigating the effect of exercise on pulse rate

Prior knowledge: None.

Advance preparation of materials: None.

Per station: Stop watch/clock.

Specific tips: If there is a medical reason why a pupil cannot exercise (see Step 3) there should be a note from the parent/guardian/GP to that effect. Pupils thus need to know what is required of them at least 24 hours in advance.

Exercise 8.10 The pulse-rate problem – *Experimental design 3*

Prior knowledge: Exercise 9.8a and b.

Advance preparation of materials: For *Procedure* stop watches/clocks

Specific tips: A problem arises if pupils wish to test subjects at home (i.e. the use of stop watches). There are 3 solutions: (a) signing for the stop watch, (b) paying a returnable deposit or (c) using a wrist watch with a sweep/digital second display. (c) is the most acceptable alternative.

SECTION 9: Sensitivity and Response

Exercises 9.1 and 9.2 require the use of Choice Chambers. Because such equipment comes in a variety of designs (albeit based on the same principles), it would be confusing to describe a single choice chamber on the candidate's worksheet. Therefore, the teacher needs to demonstrate choice chamber design and the way in which it is set up.

The cress seedlings in Exercise 9.4 need to be germinated 14 days in advance.

Exercise 9.1 Investigating the sensitivity of organisms using a choice chamber

Prior knowledge: Anhydrous calcium chloride as a drying agent.

Advance preparation of materials: Blowfly larvae/woodlice.

Per station: Choice chamber, bench lamp, white tile, blunt forceps, scissors, spatula, stop watch/clock, filter paper, beaker of water, teat pipette, cotton wool, sticky tape, black paper/card, calcium chloride, 12–15 blowfly larvae/woodlice in 'escape proof' darkened container.

Specific tips: 1. Choice chamber designs are varied, so their construction and the principles involved need to be discussed beforehand.
2. Blowfly larvae can be obtained all the year round from Angling Shops.
3. They tend to become 'light-adapted' so need to be kept in a darkened container until transferred to the choice chamber.
4. It is helpful to crush the calcium chloride crystals prior to the lesson. This reduces the chance of the crystals in the environmental chamber touching the platform when the platform is replaced.

Exercise 9.2 Which conditions? – *Experimental design 2*

Prior knowledge: Exercise 9.1.

Advance preparation of materials: For *Procedure* (i.e. available in the laboratory) apparatus and materials as per Exercise 9.1.

Exercise 9.3 Investigating the effect of light intensity on the eye

Prior knowledge: Structure of the eye.

Advance preparation of materials: None.

Per station: Bench lamp, mirror.

Exercise 9.4 Investigating the effect of light on the growth of cress plants

Prior knowledge: None.

Advance preparation of materials: Batches of cress seedlings grown in (a) light and (b) dark. Sugar paper (21 cm × 30 cm).

Per station:
(1st lesson): 2 dishes of cress seedlings (see above), 2 adhesive labels, scissors, sugar paper.
(2nd lesson): 'Screened' petri dishes of cress seedlings.

SECTION 10: Plant Reproduction and Growth

Exercises 10.1 and 10.2 are essentially the same but investigate, respectively, the flower of a wallflower (or other Crucifera) and sweet pea (or other Leguminosa). The exercise selected will depend upon the syllabus requirement of the relevant Examining Group. Exercise 10.3 assumes the observation of a hermaphroditic flower.

Exercise 10.1 Investigating flower structure and seed production (1)

Prior knowledge: Basic flower structure.

Advance preparation of materials: Cruciferae flower stalks – each stalk containing both flowers and developing seed pods.

Per station: Flower stalk, hand lens, dissecting needle, scalpel, white tile, forceps, petri dish base.

Specific tips: 1. Wallflowers are the best flowers to use.
2. Step 6 needs to be checked carefully for the presence of pollen on the anther (see mark scheme).

Exercise 10.2 Investigating flower structure and seed production (2)

Prior knowledge: Basic flower structure.

Advance preparation of materials: Leguminosae flower stalks – each stalk containing both flowers and developing seed pods.

Per station: Flower stalk, hand lens, dissecting needle, scalpel, white tile, forceps, petri dish base.

Specific tips: 1. Sweet peas are good flowers to use.
2. Step 6 – drawing of stamen: the stamens are very small and credit should be given for a reasonable attempt at the drawing. The presence of pollen on the anther needs to be checked.

Exercise 10.3 Investigating the structure of a wind-pollinated flower

Prior knowledge: Basic flower structure. Either Exercise 10.1 or 10.2.

Advance preparation of materials: Gramineae flower stalks.

Per station: Flower stalk, hand lens, black paper, white tile.

Specific tips: 1. False-oat grass flowers are the best flowers to use. The mature anthers are brown in colour and prominent.

Exercise 10.4 Investigating the structure and development (germination) of pollen grains

Prior knowledge: Either Exercise 10.1 or Exercise 10.2.

Advance preparation of materials: Flowers with ripe anthers. 10% sucrose solution.

Per station:
(1st lesson)   Microscope, bench lamp, microscope slide, white tile, beaker of water, teat pipette, chinagraph pencil, petri-dish containing 10% sucrose solution, flower stalk.
(2nd lesson)   Microscope, bench lamp, microscope slide, petri dish of sucrose solution containing pollen, teat pipette.

Specific tips: 1. Daffodil pollen germinates well in 10% sucrose solution – pollen tubes are visible after 24 hours.
2. See Exercise 4.1, tips 2 and 3.

Exercise 10.5 Investigating seed dispersal

Prior knowledge: Exercise 10.1 or Exercise 10.2.

Advance preparation of materials: Batches of the following fruits: ash, sycamore, blackberry, hawthorn, lupin, broom, wood avens, cleavers, teasel.

Per station: Examples of at least 8 fruits each of which is lettered A, B, etc., white tile, hand lens.

Specific tips: 1. 'Woody' fruits will keep for a number of years; juicy fruits need to be collected immediately prior to the lesson.
2. Any fruits can be used as long as there are at least two representatives of each method of dispersal (which conform to the mark scheme criteria).

Exercise 10.6 Investigating the structure of a seed and its food reserves

Prior knowledge: Food tests.

Advance preparation of materials: (a) Bean seeds, soaked for 24 hours prior to lesson, and (b) dry bean seeds of same species.

Per station: Bunsen burner, tripod, gauze, beaker of water, test tube rack, 2 test tubes, thermometer, scalpel, spatula, iodine solution, Benedict's solution, Biuret reagent, 1 soaked bean seed, 1 dry bean seed, white tile.

Specific tips: Syllabus specifications will govern whether broad beans or French beans should be used.

Exercises 10.7a & b Investigating what happens to the starch in a germinating seed

Prior knowledge: Starch test. Digestion of starch by amylase/carbohydrase. Digestion products. Use of sugar in aerobic respiration.

Advance preparation of materials: (a) Starch-agar plates: use agar powder. Make up solution using 0.5 parts starch, 1 part agar, 100 parts water. Mix thoroughly and heat until just boiling. Allow to cool to 45°C and pour into petri dishes. Store dishes in refrigerator until ready for use.

(b) Soak the bean seeds for 2 days. Then boil half the seeds for 15 minutes.

Per station:
(1st lesson)   Petri dish containing starch-agar, white tile, forceps, scalpel, chinagraph pencil, 2 bean seeds labelled A (boiled) and B (unboiled).
(2nd lesson)   Petri dish with bean halves, iodine solution, forceps, beaker.

Specific tips: The plates should not be left longer than 3 days before testing with iodine solution because of the action of saprophytic/parasitic fungi on the bean halves.

Exercise 10.8 The germination problem – *Experimental design 3*

Prior knowledge: Exercise 2.5 (also Exercise 8.3a – removal of dissolved oxygen from water).

Advance preparation of materials: For *Procedure* (i.e. available in the laboratory): bunsen burners, boiling tube racks, boiling tubes, test tube holders, bungs, chinagraph pencils, oil, black paper/aluminium foil, spatulas, cress seeds, (hand lenses required to obtain results).

Exercise 10.9 Investigating the growth of the stem of a French bean plant

Prior knowledge: None.

Advance preparation of materials: Potted French bean plants, each with at least 1 internode.

Per station: One potted French bean plant, chinagraph pencil, freezer bag ties.

Specific tips: 1. Exercise 10.9 (and 10.10) can be run in conjunction with Exercise 2.7 (The seed-size problem – *Experimental design*).
2. It is important that measurements are taken on a regular basis (e.g. twice a week).
3. Freezer bag ties with labels incorporated should be used.

Exercise 10.10 Investigating the growth of leaves of a French bean plant

Prior knowledge: None.

Advance preparation of materials: See Exercise 10.9.

Per station: One potted French bean plant, chinagraph pencil, freezer bag ties, graph paper (6 cm^2), card (6 cm^2).

Specific tips: 1. See tips 1, 2 and 3 of Exercise 10.9.
2. At the conclusion of this Exercise (and/or Exercise 10.9), the plants should be removed from the soil to observe the root nodules.
3. Graph paper (and card) is required in all subsequent lessons where leaf area is measured.
4. See tip 3 Exercise 10.9.

Exercise 10.11 Investigating variation in width of privet leaves

Prior knowledge: None.

Advance preparation of materials: Mature privet leaves (about 30 per station).

Per station: Approximately 30 privet leaves.

Specific tips: 1. This exercise is a good introduction to continuous variation.
2. The leaves of any other species of plant could be used – entailing the alteration of 'Leaf Width' values in the Results Table.

Chapter 7

The Mark Schemes

THEME 1 SECTION 1:   Classification/Diversity of Organisms
Exercise 1.1   Constructing a key (1)

Skills indicated by * need to be assessed during the course of the Exercise.
Candidates are not assessed on work done in this Exercise. It should be used to provide a format for subsequent assessment.

The 'branching diagram', and the key constructed from it, is a *suggested* procedure:

'Branching' diagram

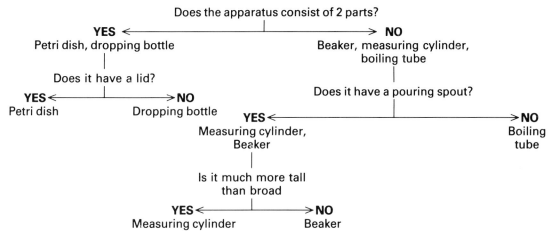

Key

1.	Consists of 2 parts	Go to 2
	Does not consist of 2 parts	Go to 3
2.	Has a lid	Petri dish
	Has no lid	Dropping bottle
3.	Has a pouring spout	Go to 4
	Has no pouring spout	Boiling tube
4.	Is much more tall than broad	Measuring cylinder
	Is not much taller than broad	Beaker

THEME 1 SECTION 1: Classification/Diversity of Organisms

Exercise 1.2 Constructing a key (2)

Skills indicated by * need to be assessed during the course of the Exercise.

*Skill area – Observation**

'Branching' diagram

Criteria	Mark	Competency Level
'Branching' diagram constructed:		
Accurately	9–7	III
With one or two minor inaccuracies	6–4	II
With (a) a major inaccuracy/and one or two minor inaccuracies (b) several minor inaccuracies	3–1	I
Skill not demonstrated	0	0

Skill area – Recording

Key

Criteria	Mark	Competency Level
Key constructed accurately from 'branching' diagram	9–7	III
Key constructed with some disorder	6–4	II
Key constructed with considerable disorder	3–1	I
Skill not demonstrated	0	0

Note

Candidates should not be penalised in the skill area *Recording* if the 'branching' diagram is inaccurate (i.e. each skill area should be assessed independently). Thus, if the key is compatible with the diagram, appropriate credit should be given. Alternatively, if the 'branching' diagram has major inaccuracies, a 'model' diagram should be supplied for the assessment of the skill area *Recording*.

THEME 1 SECTION 1: Classification/Diversity of Organisms

Exercise 1.3 Investigating the gross structure of leaves

Skills indicated by * need to be assessed during the course of the Exercise.

*Skill area – Observation**

Criteria						
Leaf	Margin	Lamina		Shape	Veins	Leaf stalk
		1	2			
A (grass)	smooth	both surfaces the same colour	both surfaces dull	long thin	parallel	hollow
B (holly)	pointed spines	upper surface dark green, lower surface light green	upper surface shiny, lower surface dull	broad	net-like	solid

1 mark for each observation. Maximum mark 9.

Mark Obtained	0	1 2 3	4 5 6	7 8 9
Competency Level	0	I	II	III

Skill area – Recording

Criteria	Mark
Vertical columns headed	1
Horizontal columns headed	1
Correct terms used for headings in vertical columns	2
At least 3 comparisons made	2
Results recorded in *single* table	1
Overall layout clear	2

Mark Obtained	0	1 2 3	4 5 6	7 8 9
Competency Level	0	I	II	III

THEME 1 SECTION 1:   Classification/Diversity of Organisms
Exercise 1.4 Leaf identification using a key

Skills indicated by * need to be assessed during the course of the Exercise.

Skill area – Observation*

Sample	Criteria			Mark
A	1, 3, 4	(1) Sycamore	($\frac{1}{2}$)	$1\frac{1}{2}$
B	1, 2	(1) Ash	($\frac{1}{2}$)	$1\frac{1}{2}$
C	1, 3, 5	(1) Privet	($\frac{1}{2}$)	$1\frac{1}{2}$
D	1, 3, 5	(1) Oak	($\frac{1}{2}$)	$1\frac{1}{2}$
E	1, 3, 4	(1) Silver birch	($\frac{1}{2}$)	$1\frac{1}{2}$
F	1, 2	(1) Horse chestnut	($\frac{1}{2}$)	$1\frac{1}{2}$

Mark Obtained	0	1	2	3	4	5	6	7	8	9
Competency Level	0		I			II			III	

THEME 1 SECTION 1:   Classification/Diversity of Organisms
Exercise 1.5 Twig identification using a key

Skills indicated by * need to be assessed during the course of the Exercise.

Skill area – Observation*

Sample	Criteria		Mark
A	1, 3, 5 (1) *Betula verrucosa* (Silver Birch)	($\frac{1}{2}$)	$1\frac{1}{2}$
B	1, 3 (1) *Quercus robur* (Oak)	($\frac{1}{2}$)	$1\frac{1}{2}$
C	1, 2, 4 (1) *Aesculus hippocastanum* (Horse Chestnut)	($\frac{1}{2}$)	$1\frac{1}{2}$
D	1, 3, 5 (1) *Crataegus sp.* (Hawthorn)	($\frac{1}{2}$)	$1\frac{1}{2}$
E	1, 2, 4 (1) *Acer pseudoplatanus* (Sycamore)	($\frac{1}{2}$)	$1\frac{1}{2}$
F	1, 2 (1) *Fraxinus excelsior* (Ash)	($\frac{1}{2}$)	$1\frac{1}{2}$

Mark Obtained	0	1	2	3	4	5	6	7	8	9
Competency Level	0		I			II			III	

THEME 1 SECTION 1: Classification/Diversity of Organisms

Exercise 1.6 Fruit identification using a key

Skills indicated by * need to be assessed during the course of the Exercise.

*Skill area – Observation**

Sample	Criteria			Mark
A	1, 2, 4	(1) *Sambucus racemosa* (Elder)	($\frac{1}{2}$)	$1\frac{1}{2}$
B	1, 3	(1) *Quercus robur* (Oak)	($\frac{1}{2}$)	$1\frac{1}{2}$
C	1, 2, 4	(1) *Crataegus sp.* (Hawthorn)	($\frac{1}{2}$)	$1\frac{1}{2}$
D	1, 3, 5	(1) *Fraxinus excelsior* (Ash)	($\frac{1}{2}$)	$1\frac{1}{2}$
E	1, 2,	(1) *Rosa sp.* (Rose)	($\frac{1}{2}$)	$1\frac{1}{2}$
F	1, 3, 5	(1) *Acer pseudoplantanus* (Sycamore)	($\frac{1}{2}$)	$1\frac{1}{2}$

Mark Obtained	0	1 2 3	4 5 6	7 8 9
Competency Level	0	I	II	III

Continued

THEME 2 SECTION 2:   Soil/Soil Improvement

Exercise 2.1 Investigating the composition of different types of soil

Skills indicated by * need to be assessed during the course of the Exercise.

Skill area – Measurement*

Volume

Criteria	Competency Level
Both volumes recorded to within $\pm$ 0.1 cm^3	III
One volume recorded to within $\pm$0.1 cm^3	II

Skill area – Observation*

Drawings

Criteria	Mark
Drawings of reasonable size in terms of space available	1
Both drawings of same size	1
At least 4 of the 5 components labelled in both tubes	2
Accurate layer depths recorded for (a) soil sample A	2
(b) soil sample B	2
Scale stated (e.g. $\times \frac{1}{3}$)	1

Mark Obtained	0	1 2 3	4 5 6	7 8 9
Competency Level	0	I	II	III

THEME 2 SECTION 2:   Soil/Soil Improvement

Exercise 2.2 Calculating the amount of water in a soil sample

Skills indicated by * need to be assessed during the course of the Exercise.

Skill area – Measurement*

Mass

Criteria	Competency Level
All masses recorded to within $\pm$ 0.1 g	III
Two masses recorded to within $\pm$ 0.1 g	II
One mass recorded to within $\pm$ 0.1 g	I

Skill area – Interpretation

Criteria	Competency Level
Calculation accomplished without assistance	III
Calculation accomplished with occasional assistance	II
Calculation accomplished with regular assistance	I
Unable to accomplish calculation/calculation not attempted	0

THEME 2 SECTION 2: Soil/Soil Improvement

Exercise 2.3a Calculating the amount of humus in a soil sample

Skills indicated by * need to be assessed during the course of the Exercise.

Skill area – Measurement*

Mass

Criteria	Competency Level
Mass measurement to within ± 0.1 g	III
Mass measurement outside ± 0.1 g	0

Skill area – Manipulation*

Criteria	Mark
Stable set-up of pipe-clay triangle and crucible	2
Bunsen burner adjusted for 'roaring' flame	1
Lid (except for short periods) kept on crucible throughout heating	1
Safe and careful removal of lid during heating	2
Lid placed on heat-resistant mat after heating	1
Sensible testing of hot crucible prior to removal for weighing	2

Mark Obtained	0	1	2	3	4	5	6	7	8	9
Competency Level	0		I			II			III	

Skill area – Interpretation

Criteria	Competency Level
Calculation accomplished without assistance	III
Calculation accomplished with occasional assistance	I
Calculation accomplished with regular assistance	I
Unable to accomplish calculation/calculation not attempted	0

THEME 2 SECTION 2:   Soil/Soil Improvement

Exercise 2.3b   Interpreting the results of Exercises 2.2 and 2.3a

Skills indicated by * need to be assessed during the course of the Exercise.

Skill area – Interpretation

Question	Criteria	Mark
1.	So there are no complications (e.g. loss of material) in the transfer of the dry soil to a heat-proof container for the 'burning off' of the humus in Exercise 2.3a.	1
2.	A crucible is heat-proof and will not crack at high temperatures.	1
3.	The soil is heated to a higher temperature because bunsen flame is directed on to base of crucible.	1
4.	To prevent soil particles spurting out of the crucible (1) and so leading to an inaccurate result on subsequent weighing (1).	2
5.	Both humus *and* water would otherwise be lost during burning.	1
6.	By heating and reweighing, in each case, until 2 weighings give the same result.	2
7. (a) (b)	Clay soil ($\frac{1}{2}$) Sandy soil ($\frac{1}{2}$)	1

Mark Obtained	0	1 2 3	4 5 6	7 8 9
Competency Level	0	I	II	III

THEME 2 SECTION 2: Soil/Soil Improvement

Exercise 2.4 Collecting and observing nematode worms (round worms) from a soil sample

Skills indicated by * need to be assessed during the course of the Exercise.

Skill area – Following Instructions*

Criteria	Mark	Competency Level
Steps 1–7 followed *without assistance*. Procedures carried out *competently* and *safely*.	9–7	III
Steps 1–7 followed and procedures carried out with *occasional assistance*. Shows *awareness* of safety precautions but is *sometimes careless*.	6–4	II
Steps 1–7 followed and procedures carried out only with *regular/ constant supervision*. Uses safety precautions *only when reminded*.	3–1	I
Incapable of following Steps 1–7 and carrying out procedures, *or* skill not attempted	0	0

Skill area – Manipulation*

Microscope adjustment

Criteria	Mark
Mirror adjusted for optimum clarity	3
Condenser adjusted for optimum clarity	3
Microscope focused for optimum clarity	3

Mark Obtained	0	1	2	3	4	5	6	7	8	9
Competency Level	0		I			II			III	

THEME 2 SECTION 2: Soil/Soil Improvement

Exercise 2.5 Technology – Investigating the effect of adding lime to a clay soil

Skills indicated by * need to be assessed during the course of the Exercise.

Skill area – Measurement*

Volume

Criteria	Competency Level
Both volume measurements to within $\pm$ 0.1 cm^3	III
One volume measurement to within $\pm$0.1 cm^3	II

Skill area – Observation*

Initial observation (Step 3)

Tube	Criteria	Mark
A (water)	Clay remains suspended in water (1) Slight clearing towards water surface (1)	2
B (limewater)	Clay particles clump together (2) and fall to bottom of boiling tube (1)	3

Final observation (Step 4)

Tube	Criteria	Mark
A (water)	Shallow layer of clay at bottom of boiling tube (1) Liquid above layer of clay is opaque (1)	2
B (limewater)	Deep layer of clay at bottom of boiling tube (1) Liquid above layer of clay is almost clear (1)	2

Mark Obtained	0	1 2 3	4 5 6	7 8 9
Competency Level	0	I	II	III

Answer to Step 5 (not for assessment)
Lime causes clay particles to stick together in 'clumps'. This increases the air space in the soil so that it drains better and does not become water-logged.

THEME 2 SECTION 2:   Soil/Soil Improvement

Exercise 2.6 Hydroponics – Germinating cress seeds to use in investigations into plant growth

Skills indicated by * need to be assessed during the course of the Exercise.

Skill area – Measurement*

Criteria	Competency Level
All volumes measurements to within $\pm$ 0.1 cm^3	III
1 volume measurement *not* within $\pm$ 0.1 cm^3	II
2 volumes measurement *not* within $\pm$ 0.1 cm^3	I

Skill area – Manipulation*

Criteria	Mark
Labels fixed according to instructions (Step 1)	1
Correct amount of Perlite added to each petri dish (1) with minimum spillage (1), and flattened (1)	3
Volumes of water added to Perlite in each petri dish such that: Perlite moistened (1) No standing water (1)	2
Cress seeds: Evenly spread in each dish (1) Evenly distributed between dishes (1) Pressed into surface of Perlite (1)	3

Mark Obtained	0	1 2 3	4 5 6	7 8 9
Competency Level	0	I	II	III

THEME 2 SECTION 2:   Soil/Soil Improvement

Exercise 2.7   The seed-size problem – *Experimental design 3*

Skills indicated by * need to be assessed during the course of the Exercise.

Skill area – Experimental design

All skills within the skill area *Experimental design* (with the exception of the skill *Recording*) are marked using the following rating scale:

Criteria	Mark	Competency Level
Skill accomplished with no assistance	9–7	III
Skill accomplished with occasional assistance	6–4	II
Skill accomplished with regular assistance	3–1	I
Incapable of accomplishing skill	0	0

Skill – Problem identification/Hypothesis formulation
General criterion: Can identify problem/formulate a hypothesis.

Specific criteria for this Exercise:

1. A greater mass of seeds, per plant, is produced.

2. *Do plants grown from large seeds produce a greater mass of seeds than those grown from small seeds?

3. Large pea seeds produce plants which have a greater mass of seeds than plants grown from small pea seeds.

*Because we are dealing with *crop* plants, the *mass* of seed produced is the critical factor rather than the *size* of plant.

Skill – Apparatus selection
General criterion: Can select appropriate apparatus.

Specific criteria for this Exercise:

>   Growing medium (e.g. potting compost)
>   Containers for seed sowing
>   Batch of named seeds
>   Instrument for determining seed size (ruler/balance)

Skill – Planning
General criterion: Can produce logical, staged plan of the experiment.

Specific criteria for this Exercise:

1. Stated criterion for selecting small/large seeds of stated plant (e.g. seeds over/under a certain length/mass).

2. Stated number of seeds sown (e.g. 30 per batch).

3. *Seeds sown* at same time, in different containers under identical conditions (i.e. growing medium, volume of water added, seed spacing and depth, temperature).

4. *After germination*, plants placed in areas of same light intensity, watered equally.

5. Prior to flower formation, a stated method of preventing cross-pollination between the two batches of plants (e.g. polythene bags/transfer one batch to a separate area).

6. Collect seeds, as pods ripen, each week. Weigh and record.

Skill – Procedure*

General criterion: Can follow plan competently and safely.

Skill – Recording

Specific criteria for this Exercise:

Plants	Mass of seeds collected (g)					
	Week 1	Week 2	Week 3	Week 4	Total	Mean mass of seeds produced per plant
Grown from small seeds						
Grown from large seeds						

Criteria	Mark
Vertical columns headed	1
Horizontal columns headed	1
Units stated (mass, g)	1
Full set of results recorded	1
Means recorded	1
No anomalous results, or anomalous results noted and eliminated	1
Results recorded in a *single* table	1
Overall layout clear	2

Mark Obtained	0	1 2 3	4 5 6	7 8 9
Competency Level	0	I	II	III

Skill – Interpretaton
General criterion: Can reach appropriate conclusions and identify patterns.

Specific criteria for this Exercise:

1. Results give a direct comparison of the crop produced in each case.

2. Hypothesis confirmed or, if rejected, a new hypothesis formulated.

Skill – Evaluation
General criterion: Can recognise limitations of method/method improvement/area of future study.

Specific criteria for this Exercise:

1. Limitations of method – problems associated with conducting experiments over a long period of time. Controlled pollination could effect seed production.

2. Future study:

    (a) Many plants produce only very small seeds. Does the size of the seed limit the size of the mature plant?

    (b) Do plants grown for their flowers produce bigger blooms if only the largest seeds are sown?

THEME 2 SECTION 2:   Soil/Soil Improvement

Exercise 2.8a Technology – Investigating the lack of certain chemical elements on the growth of cress plants

Skills indicated by * need to be assessed during the course of the Exercise.

Skill area – Following instructions*

Criteria	Mark	Competency Level
Instructions Steps 1–6 followed *without assistance*. Procedures carried out *competently* and *safely*.	9–7	III
Instructions Steps 1–6 followed and procedures carried out with *occasional assistance*. Shows *awareness* of safety precautions but *sometimes careless*.	6–4	II
Instructions Steps 1–6 followed and procedures carried out only with *regular/constant supervision*. Uses safety precautions *only when reminded*.	3–1	I
Incapable of following instructions Steps 1–6 and carrying out procedures, *or* skill not attempted	0	0

Skill area – Recording

Criteria	Mark
Table 1: Full set of results entered	1
Mean for each set of results entered	1
Mean recorded to nearest whole number	1
Length expressed in mm	1
Table 2: Leaf colour recorded for all batches	1
At least *one* other observation recorded	1

Maximum Competency Level = II

Mark obtained	0	1 2 3	4 5 6
Comptetency Level	0	I	II

THEME 2 SECTION 2:   Soil/Soil Improvement

Exercise 2.8b   Interpreting the results of Exercise 2.8a

Skills indicated by * need to be assessed during the course of the Exercise.

Skill area – Interpretation

Question		Criteria	Mark
1.		Complete culture	1
2.	(a)	No	1
	(b)	There is not a great enough difference between the mean root lengths (2 mm) (1). More evidence (e.g. dry mass, leaf size, presence of lateral roots, stem length) would be required before a positive statement could be made (1)	2
3.	(a)	Proteins	1
	(b)	Growth	1
	(c)	Production/synthesis of green colour/green pigment/ chlorophyll in the leaves	1
4.		Carbon is taken into plants through the leaves (1) as carbon dioxide (1)	2

Mark Obtained	0	1	2	3	4	5	6	7	8	9
Competency Level	0		I			II			III	

Continued

THEME 2 SECTION 3: Bacteriology

Exercise 3.1 Preparing a petri dish for growing bacteria

Skills indicated by * need to be assessed during the course of the Exercise.

Skill area – Following instructions*

Criteria	Mark	Competency Level
Instructions followed *without assistance*. Procedures carried out *competently* and *safely*.	9–7	III
Instructions followed and procedures carried out with *occasional assistance*. Shows *awareness* of safety precautions but is *sometimes careless*.	6–4	II
Instructions followed and procedures carried out only with *regular/constant supervision*. Uses safety precautions *only when* reminded.	3–1	I
Incapable of following Instructions and carrying out procedures, *or* skill *not* attempted	0	0

Skill area – Interpretation

Sterile technique	Criteria (i) and (ii)	Mark
(a) Wipe hands	Destroy bacteria on skin surface	1
(b) Wipe bench	Destroy bacteria in dust, etc. on bench	1
(c) Do not remove petri dish lid	Prevent air-borne bacteria contaminating agar	1
(d) 'Flame' bottle mouth	Destroy, by heat, bacteria on bottle mouth	1
(e) Pour quickly	Reduce chance of air-borne bacteria contaminating agar	1
(f) Replace lid immediately	As for (e)	1
(g) Rewipe hands	Personal safety precaution	1
(h) Leave petri dish	Liquid agar may spill and be contaminated by bacteria in air, on bench, on hands, etc.	2

Mark Obtained	0	1	2	3	4	5	6	7	8	9
Competency Level	0		I			II			III	

THEME 2 SECTION 3: Bacteriology

Exercise 3.2 Infecting nutrient agar with a solution in which bacteria are suspected of being present

Skills indicated by * need to be assessed during the course of the Exercise.

Skill area – Manipulation*

Criteria	Mark
Bunsen adjusted correctly for 'roaring' flame	1
Whole of wire of inoculating loop heated safely	2
No spillage of solution on transfer to agar	2
Petri dish lid lifted for minimum operational time	2
Streak is over 'contaminated' area only	2

Mark Obtained	0	1 2 3	4 5 6	7 8 9
Competency Level	0	I	II	III

Skill area – Interpretation

Question	Criteria	Mark
1.	Swab bench, clean hands – no mark (repetition of techniques in Exercise 5.1)	
	Heat inoculating loop Lid off petri dish for minimum time Lid sellotaped to base	1 1 1
2.	To ensure that the results for the *contaminated* agar are due to the transfer from the suspected solution and not to some other cause arising from faulty sterile technique	3
3.	At 0°C, bacteria would only grow and multiply very slowly At 100°C, bacteria (i) would be destroyed (ii) would probably be destroyed	1 either 1 or 2

Mark Obtained	0	1 2 3	4 5 6	7 8 9
Competency Level	0	I	II	III

THEME 2 SECTION 3:   Bacteriology
Exercise 3.3   The growth of bacteria on nutrient agar

Skills indicated by * need to be assessed during the course of the Exercise.

Skill area – Observation*

Criteria	Mark
All growths drawn	2
Growth in correct relative positions	2
Growths in correct proportions to others and to the dish	2
Drawing lines neat, clear, distinct	2
Growths labelled as accurately as observation allows	1

Mark Obtained	0	1 2 3	4 5 6	7 8 9
Competency Level	0	I	II	III

Skill area – Measurement*

NB Area of base of standard petri dish $= 60 \text{ cm}^2$

(a)

Area of nutrient agar	Competency Level
+ or − 2% error	III
+ or − 5% error	II
+ or − 10% error	I
Grossly inaccurate	0

(b)

Area of contamination	Competency Level
+ or − 2% error	III
+ or − 5% error	II
+ or − 10% error	I
Grossly inaccurate	0

THEME 2 SECTION 3:   Bacteriology
Exercise 3.4   The milk-souring problem – *Experimental design 3*

Skills indicated by * need to be assessed during the course of the Exercise.

Skill area – Experimental design 3

All skills within the skill area *Experimental design* (with the exception of the skill *Recording*) are marked using the following rating scale:

Criteria	Mark	Competency Level
Skill accomplished with no assistance	9–7	III
Skill accomplished with occasional assistance	6–4	II
Skill accomplished with regular assistance	3–1	I
Incapable of accomplishing skill	0	0

Skill – Problem identification/hypothesis formulation

General criterion: Can identify problem/formulate a hypothesis.

Specific criteria for this Exercise:

1. (a) Bacteria
   (b) Bacteria changing lactose to lactic acid.

2. (a) Slow down their rate of growth
   (b) Increase their rate of growth

3. Does milk, left in warm conditions, contain large numbers of bacteria? (Does refrigerated milk contain few bacteria?)

4. Bacteria grow/multiply quicker at warmer temperatures, causing the milk to turn sour. (Bacteria grow/multiply slower at low temperatures causing the milk to stay fresh.)

Skill – Apparatus selection

General criterion: Can select appropriate apparatus.

Specific criteria for this Exercise:

Apparatus required: Petri dish of nutrient agar — Chinagraph pencil
Disinfectant — Black paper square
Cotton wool — Acetate sheet square
Bunsen burner — Fresh (refrigerated) milk
Inoculating loop — Sour milk

Skill – Planning

General criterion: Can produce a logical, staged plan of an experiment with, where appropriate, controls.

Specific criteria for this Exercise:

1. Steps 1 to 5 of Exercise 3.2 (half the agar streaked with fresh milk, half streaked with sour milk).

2. Steps 1 to 4 of Exercise 3.3.

Some indication of replication is required.

Skill – Procedure*

General criterion: Can follow plan competently and safely.

Specific criteria for this Exercise: Safety (i.e. sterile technique) is a feature which requires careful supervision. Correct technique should be credited accordingly.

Skill – Recording

Specific criteria for this Exercise:

Exercise 3.3 Step 4 (percentage areas of contamination unnecessary as equal areas of agar were streaked).

Results table

Sample	Area of nutrient agar contaminated (cm^2)
Fresh milk	
Sour milk	

Criteria	Mark
Vertical columns headed	1
Horizontal columns headed	1
Units (cm^2) recorded	1
Two sets of results recorded	1
Area of contamination calculated and recorded correctly	2
Results recorded in *single* table	1
Overall layout clear	2

Mark Obtained	0	1	2	3	4	5	6	7	8	9
Competency Level	0		I			II			III	

Skill – Interpretation

General criterion: Can reach appropriate conclusions and identify patterns.

Specific criteria for this Exercise: If the areas streaked were identical, the relative contamination by bacterial colonies gives results by which the hypothesis can either be confirmed or rejected.

If rejected, another hypothesis is formulated.

Skill – Evaluation

General criterion: Can recognise limitations of method/method improvement/areas of future study.

Specific criterion for this Exercise: Limitations of method/method improvement, e.g. improved sterile technique.

THEME 4.2 SECTION 3:   Bacteriology

Exercise 3.5 Biotechnology – Designing an experiment to isolate and grow a specific bacterial colony from a petri dish of nutrient agar containing a number of different types of colony – *Experimental design 1*

Skills indicated by * need to be assessed during the course of the Exercise.

Skill area – Experimental design 1

All skills within the skill area *Experimental design* (with the exception of the skill *Recording*) are marked using the following rating scale:

Criteria	Mark	Competency Level
Skill accomplished with no assistance	9–7	III
Skill accomplished with occasional assistance	6–4	II
Skill accomplished with regular assistance	3–1	I
Incapable of accomplishing skill	0	0

Skill – Apparatus selection

General criterion: Can select appropriate apparatus.

Specific criteria for this Exercise:

Additional apparatus required: Innoculating loop
                                Bunsen burner
                                Cotton wool
                                Disinfectant

Skill – Planning

General criterion: Can produce a logical, staged plan of an experiment with, where appropriate, controls.

Specific criteria for this Exercise:

1. Heat innoculating loop, cool.
2. Use loop to pick up part of Colony X.
3. Streak whole surface of nutrient agar in sterile petri dish.
4. Transfer to oven at 37°C until colonies cover surface of nutrient agar.

Sterile techniques: Disinfect hands and bench.
                     Lift lid of petri dish for minimal operation time.
                     Tape lid to base.

THEME 3 SECTION 4: Cell Structure

Exercise 4.1 Examining onion cells using a microscope

Skills indicated by * need to be assessed during the course of the Exercise.

Skill area – Manipulation *

1. Slide preparation

Criteria	Mark
Material removed effectively from its source	1
Area of material less than that of cover slip	1
All material covered by cover slip	1
Tissue smooth and flat	1
Cover slip placed using correct technique	1
No excess iodine solution on slide	2
No air bubbles	2

Mark Obtained	0	1 2 3	4 5 6	7 8 9
Competency Level	0	I	II	III

2. Microscope adjustment

Criteria	Mark
Mirror adjusted for optimum clarity	3
Condenser adjusted for optimum clarity	3
Microscope focused for optimum clarity	3

Mark Obtained	0	1 2 3	4 5 6	7 8 9
Competency Level	0	I	II	III

Skill area – Observation *

Criteria	Mark
Cells drawn identifiable from slide	2
Drawings of a reasonable size in terms of the space available	2
Cells and contents (e.g. nuclei) in correct proportions	1
Cell structures labelled as accurately as observation allows (nucleus, cytoplasm, cell wall, vacuole)	1
Drawing lines neat, clear, distinct	2
Scale stated (e.g. × 400)	1

Mark Obtained	0	1 2 3	4 5 6	7 8 9
Competency Level	0	I	II	III

THEME 3 SECTION 4:   Cell Structure

Exercise 4.2   Examining rhubarb stalk epidermal cells using a microscope

Skills indicated by * need to be assessed during the course of the Exercise.

Skill area – Manipulation*

1. Slide preparation

Criteria	Mark
Material removed effectively from its source	2
Area of material less than that of cover slip	1
All material covered by cover slip	1
Cover slip placed using correct technique	1
No excess iodine solution on slide	2
No air bubbles	2

Mark Obtained	0	1 2 3	4 5 6	7 8 9
Competency Level	0	I	II	III

2. Microscope adjustment

Criteria	Mark
Mirror adjusted for optimum clarity	3
Condenser adjusted for optimum clarity	3
Microscope focused for optimum clarity	3

Mark Obtained	0	1 2 3	4 5 6	7 8 9
Competency Level	0	I	II	III

Skill area – Observation*

Criteria	Mark
Cells drawn identifiable from slide	2
Drawings of a reasonable size in terms of the space available	2
Cells and contents (e.g. nuclei) in correct proportions	1
Cell structures labelled as accurately as observation allows (nucleus, cytoplasm, cell wall, vacuole)	1
Drawing lines neat, clear, distinct	2
Scale stated (e.g. × 400)	1

Mark Obtained	0	1　2　3	4　5　6	7　8　9
Competency Level	0	I	II	III

THEME 3 SECTION 4:　Cell Structure

Exercise 4.3　Examining human cheek cells using a microscope

Skills indicated by * need to be assessed during the course of the Exercise.

Skill area – Manipulation*

1. Slide preparation

Criteria	Mark
Material removed effectively from its source	2
Material placed centrally	1
Iodine solution added over correct area	1
Cover slip placed using correct technique	1
No excess iodine solution on slide	2
No air bubbles	2

Mark Obtained	0	1　2　3	4　5　6	7　8　9
Competency Level	0	I	II	III

2. *Microscope adjustment*

Criteria	Mark
Mirror adjusted for optimum clarity	3
Condenser adjusted for optimum clarity	3
Microscope focused for optimum clarity	3

Mark Obtained	0	1 2 3	4 5 6	7 8 9
Competency Level	0	I	II	III

Skill area – Observation*

Criteria	Mark
Cells drawn identifiable from slide	2
Drawings of a reasonable size in terms of the space available	2
Cells and contents (e.g. nuclei) in correct proportions	1
Cell structures labelled as accurately as observation allows (nucleus, cytoplasm, cell membrane)	1
Drawing lines neat, clear, distinct	2
Scale state (e.g. × 400)	1

Mark Obtained	0	1 2 3	4 5 6	7 8 9
Competency Level	0	I	II	III

Continued

THEME 3 SECTION 4:   Cell Structure

Exercise 4.4 Examining the leaf cells of Canadian pond weed using a microscope

Skills indicated by * need to be assessed during the course of the Exercise.

Skill area – Manipulation*

1. Slide preparation

Criteria	Mark
Upper surface of leaf resting on base of cavity	1
Correct volume of water added to cavity	2
Cover slip placed centrally over cavity	1
Cover slip placed using correct technique	1
No excess water on slide	2
No air bubbles	2

Mark Obtained	0	1 2 3	4 5 6	7 8 9
Competency Level	0	I	II	III

2. Microscope adjustment

Criteria	Mark
Mirror adjusted for optimum clarity	3
Condenser adjusted for optimum clarity	3
Microscope focused for optimum clarity	3

Mark Obtained	0	1 2 3	4 5 6	7 8 9
Competency Level	0	I	II	III

*Skill area – Observation**

Criteria	Mark
Cells drawn identifiable from slide	2
Drawing of reasonable size in terms of space available	2
Chloroplast labelled correctly	1
Chloroplasts in correct proportions to cell	1
Drawing lines neat, clear, distinct	2
Scale stated (e.g. × 400)	1

Mark Obtained	0	1 2 3	4 5 6	7 8 9
Competency Level	0	I	II	III

Continued

THEME 3 SECTION 5:   Nutrition and Digestion

Exercise 5.1 Testing food to see if the nutrients starch, protein and glucose are present

Skills indicated by * need to be assessed during the course of the Exercise.

Skill area – Observation*

Test using	Part marks for colour changes observed	Mark
Iodine solution	From white (1) to dark (1) blue (1)	3
Biuret reagent	From white (1) to lilac (1)	2
Benedict's solution	From white (1) to light blue ($\frac{1}{2}$) to green (1) to yellow ($\frac{1}{2}$) to orange (1)	4

Mark Obtained	0	1 2 3	4 5 6	7 8 9
Competency Level	0	I	II	III

Skill area – Manipulation*

Criteria	Mark
Bunsen remains alight throughout test	1
Low, blue flame maintained	1
Flame controlled using air hole and gas tap	1
Sensible technique for cooling water if temperature rises above 40°C (e.g. adding cold water)	1

Frequent temperature checks:
     with thermometer *in* the water
     but raised off base of beaker
	1
	1
	1

Temperature of water maintained between 35°C and 40°C throughout the test	2

Mark Obtained	0	1 2 3	4 5 6	7 8 9
Competency Level	0	I	II	III

THEME 3 SECTION 5:   Nutrition and Digestion

Exercise 5.2   Investigating plaque on teeth

Skills indicated by * need to be assessed during the course of the Exercise.

*Skill area – Observation**

Drawing	Criteria	Mark
Uncleaned teeth	(a) Heavy shading in teeth/gum area (b) Heavy shading between teeth (c) Lighter shading over teeth surface	3
Teeth cleaned from side to side	Reduction in shading of (a), (b) and (c)	3
Teeth cleaned up and down	Considerable reduction in shading. Some light shading in teeth/gum area and between teeth	3

Mark Obtained	0	1 2 3	4 5 6	7 8 9
Competency Level	0	I	II	III

y*

1

Recording
44*Graph*

Criteria	Mark
Sensible scale	2
Time on x axis	1
x axis labelled *Time* (*mins*)	2
y axis labelled *pH*	1
Points plotted accurately*	1
Points joined accurately*	1
Graph given a suitable title	1

*A mark *must* be obtained for each of these criteria for Competency Level III

Mark Obtained	0	1 2 3	4 5 6	7 8 9
Competency Level	0	I	II	III

99

Skill area – Interpretation

Question	Criteria	Mark
1.	7.2	1
2.	pH level drops – becomes more acid	1
3.	2 minutes	1
4.	23.5 minutes	1
5.	All sugar-containing foods are eaten at one time and so the pH level in the mouth is at a dangerous level for only short periods each day	2
6.	Sweets contain a high level of sugar which is responsible for producing plaque. Crisps, fruit and nuts contain little or no sugar	2
7.	Bacteria	1

Mark Obtained	0	1 2 3	4 5 6	7 8 9
Competency Level	0	I	II	III

THEME 3 SECTION 5:   Nutrition and Digestion

Exercise 5.3a Investigating the digestion of egg white

Skills indicated by * need to be assessed during the course of the Exercise.

Skill area – Manipulation*

Criteria	Mark
Bunsen remains alight throughout Exercise	1
Low, blue flame maintained	1
Flame controlled using air-hole collar and gas tap	1
Sensible technique for cooling water if temperature rises above 40°C (e.g. adding cold water)	1
Frequent temperature checks:	1
with thermometer in the water	1
but raised off base of beaker	1
Temperature of water maintained between 35°C and 40°C throughout Exercise	2

Mark Obtained	0	1 2 3	4 5 6	7 8 9
Competency Level	0	I	II	III

Skill area – Following instructions*

Criteria	Mark	Competency Level
Steps 2–6 followed *without assistance*. Procedures carried out *competently* and *safely*.	9–7	III
Steps 2–6 followed and procedures carried out with *occasional assistance*. Shows *awareness* of safety precautions but *sometimes careless*.	6–4	II
Steps 2–6 followed and procedures carried out only with *regular/ constant supervision*. Uses safety precautions *only when reminded*.	3–1	I
Incapable of following Steps 2–6 and carrying out procedures *or* skill *not attempted*.	0	0

THEME 3 SECTION 5: Nutrition and Digestion

Exercise 5.3b Interpreting the results of Exercise 5.3a

Skills indicated by * need to be assessed during the course of the Exercise.

Skill area – Interpretation

Question	Criteria	Mark
1.	A	1
2.	Dissolved/made soluble (*not* disappeared)	1
3.	Acid, protease	2
4.	No protease present	2
5. (a)	Yes	1
(b)	Solutions alkaline/no acid present so protease cannot work	2

Mark Obtained	0	1	2	3	4	5	6	7	8	9
Competency Level	0		I			II			III	

THEME 3 SECTION 5:   Nutrition and Digestion

Exercise 5.4a Investigating the effect of amylase on starch

Skills indicated by * need to be assessed during the course of the Exercise.

Skill area – Following instructions*

Criteria	Mark	Competency Level
Instructions followed *without assistance*. Procedures carried out *competently* and *safely*.	9–7	III
Instructions followed and procedures carried out with *occasional assistance*. Shows *awareness* of safety precautions but *sometimes careless*.	6–4	II
Instructions followed and procedures carried out only with *regular/ constant supervision*. Uses safety precautions *only when reminded*.	3–1	I
Incapable of following instructions and carrying out procedures *or* skill not attempted.	0	0

Skill area – Measurement*

Criteria	Competency Level
Volume measurement to within $\pm\ 0.1\ cm^3$	III
Volume measurement outside $\pm\ 0.1\ cm^3$	0

Skill area – Recording

Results table

Time (min)	Colour produced with iodine solution:	
	Solution in test tube A (starch and boiled amylase)	Solution in test tube B (starch and unboiled amylase)
0	dark blue	dark blue
5	dark blue	blue/lilac
10	dark blue	light brown
15	dark blue	light brown

Criteria	Mark
Vertical columns headed	1
Horizontal columns headed	1
Units of time (min) stated	1
Time commences at 0 mins	1
Full set of results recorded	1
Colours accurately recorded	1
Results recorded in *single* table	1
Overall layout clear	2

Mark Obtained	0	1 2 3	4 5 6	7 8 9
Competency Level	0	I	II	III

THEME 3 SECTION 5:   Nutrition and Digestion

Exercise 5.4b Interpreting the results of Exercise 5.4a

Skills indicated by * need to be assessed during the course of the Exercise.

Skill area – Interpretation

Question	Criteria	Mark
1. (a)	Because starch was present	1
(b)	The absence of starch	1
2.	Amylase was destroyed (denatured) by boiling and so could not break down the starch	1
3. (a)	Starch is changed into something else (1) by the action of amylase (1)	2
(b)	Add Benedict's solution to a sample of the solution in test tube B (1). Warm in water bath for 5 minutes (1)	2
4.	A 3rd test tube containing 2 cm^3 starch and 2 cm^3 *water* (1). Test with iodine solution at 5 minute intervals (1)	2

Mark Obtained	0	1 2 3	4 5 6	7 8 9
Competency Level	0	I	II	III

THEME 3 SECTION 5:   Nutrition and Digestion

Exercise 5.5 Find the enzyme – *Experimental design 2*

Skills indicated by * need to be assessed during the course of the Exercise.

Skill area – Experimental design 2

All skills within the skill area *Experimental design* (with the exception of the skill *Recording*) are marked using the following rating scale:

Criteria	Mark	Competency Level
Skill accomplished with no assistance	9–7	III
Skill accomplished with occasional assistance	6–4	II
Skill accomplished with regular assistance	3–1	I
Incapable of accomplishing skill	0	0

Skill – Apparatus selection

General criterion: Can select appropriate apparatus.

Specific criteria for this Exercise:

Apparatus required:	Clean test tubes	Stop clock/watch
	Test tube rack	2 dropping pipettes
	Water bath	Chinagraph pencil
	Spotting tile	Reagent: Iodine solution

Skill – Planning

General criterion: Can produce a logical staged plan of an experiment.

Specific criteria for this Exercise:

1. Pour 2 cm³ of A, B and C into 3 separate test tubes. Add 2 drops of iodine solution to each. Note the solution which causes the iodine solution to turn dark blue. This is starch solution (assume solution A). Record.

2. Divide the remainder of solution A into two equal volumes by pouring half into a clean test tube. Using a chinagraph pencil, label one test tube 'A + B', and the other 'A + C'.

3. Add 3 cm³ of solution B to the test tube labelled 'A + B'. Add 3 cm³ of solution C to the test tube labelled 'A + C'.

4. Put both test tubes in a water bath (37°C).

5. Add drops of iodine solution to the dimples on each side of the spotting tile. Label one side 'A + B' and the other 'A + C'.

6. Using separate pipettes, test each solution for the presence of starch every 2 minutes until one set of iodine drops fails to produce a dark blue colour. Record results in table. The solution added to these iodine drops contains glucose and amylase (i.e. the amylase has converted the starch to glucose). By a process of elimination, the other solution must be glucose.

Skill – Procedure*

Specific criterion for this Exercise: Plan (above) followed competently and safely.

Skill – Recording

Results table

Time (min)	Appearance after adding iodine solution	
	Solutions A + B	Solutions A + C
0		
2		
4		
6		
8		

Criteria	Mark
Vertical columns headed	1
Horizontal columns headed	1
Unit of time (min) stated	1
Full set of results recorded	1
Results recorded in *single* table	1
Overall layout clear	2
Contents of solutions A, B and C recorded below table	2

Mark Obtained	0	1	2	3	4	5	6	7	8	9
Competency Level	0		I			II			III	

THEME 3 SECTION 5: Nutrition and Digestion
Exercise 5.6a Demonstrating a 'model gut'

Skills indicated by * need to be assessed during the course of the Exercise.

Skill area – Manipulation*

Criteria	Mark
Visking tubing $\frac{3}{4}$ filled with no leakage/spillage	2
Tubing rinsed thoroughly	1
Step 6 carried out competently	2
Step 7 carried out competently, with reference to the drawing	1
Step 8 carried out competently Step 9 carried out competently	3

Mark Obtained	0	1 2 3	4 5 6	7 8 9
Competency Level	0	I	II	III

THEME 3 SECTION 5: Nutrition and Digestion
Exercise 5.6b Interpreting the results of Exercise 5.6a

Skills indicated by * need to be assessed during the course of the Exercise.

Skill area – Interpretation

Question		Criteria	Mark
1.		37°C is the normal body temperature.	1
2.		To remove any starch/glucose solution that may have accidentally been pipetted on to the outside of the Visking tubing.	1
3.		To ensure that the starch/glucose solution cannot seep out of the paper-clipped end into the water in the boiling tube.	1
4.	(a)	It allows small glucose molecules to pass through (1) but not large starch molecules (1).	2
	(b)	Only soluble nutrients can pass through the gut wall and into the bloodstream.	1
5.		Tissue fluid/blood	1
6.		*Examples:* no villi present no peristalsis	1 1

Mark Obtained	0	1	2	3	4	5	6	7	8	9
Competency Level	0		I			II			III	

ut competently

Step 7

THEME 3 SECTION 5:   Nutrition and Digestion

Exercise 5.7 Demonstrating digestion and absorption of a carbohydrate

Skills indicated by * need to be assessed during the course of the Exercise.

*Skill area – Manipulation**

Criteria	Mark
Visking tubing $\frac{3}{4}$ filled with no leakage/spillage	2
Tubing rinsed thoroughly	1
Step 6 carried out competently	2
Step 7 carried out competently, with reference to the drawing	1
Step 8 carried out competently } Step 9 carried out competently	3

Mark Obtained	0	1	2	3	4	5	6	7	8	9
Competency Level	0		I			II			III	

THEME 3 SECTION 5:   Nutrition and Digestion

Exercise 5.8a Investigating the effect of bile salts on cooking oil

Skills indicated by * need to be assessed during the course of the Exercise.

Skill area – Following instructions*

Criteria	Mark	Competency Level
Instructions followed *without assistance*. Procedures carried out *competently* and *safely*.	9–7	III
Instructions followed and procedures carried out with *occasional assistance*. Shows *awareness* of safety precautions but *sometimes careless*.	6–4	II
Instructions followed and procedures carried out only with *regular/constant supervision*. Uses safety precautions *only when reminded*.	3–1	I
Incapable of following instructions and carrying out procedures, *or* skill not attempted	0	0

Skill area – Observation*

Test tube	Hand lens observation	Naked eye observation	Mark
1	Large globules/blobs (2)	Oil and water separates (1)	3
2	Very small, fine 'particles' (2)	dense, yellowish 'mixture' (1)	3
3	Very small, fine 'particles' (2)	dense, yellowish 'mixture' (1)	3

Mark Obtained	0	1 2 3	4 5 6	7 8 9
Competency Level	0	I	II	III

THEME 3 SECTION 5:   Nutrition and Digestion
Exercise 5.8b   Interpreting the results of Exercise 5.8a

Skills indicated by * need to be assessed during the course of the Exercise.

Skill area – Interpretation

Question	Criteria	Mark
1.	It cannot break down grease into small globules	1
2.	It increases the surface area of the fat (1) so that fat-digesting enzyme (lipase) can 'attack' the fat much more easily (1)	2
3.	Lipase breaks down fat into even smaller parts (1 mark only). Lipase chemically breaks down fat	2
4.	Fried fish ($\frac{1}{2}$) Steak ($\frac{1}{2}$) Butter ($\frac{1}{2}$) Full cream milk ($\frac{1}{2}$) } (1 mark deducted for each incorrect answer. Minimum mark 0)	2
5.	All have a high fat content (1). Absence of bile means no emulsification and so fat will be only partially digested (1)	2

Mark Obtained	0	1 2 3	4 5 6	7 8 9
Competency Level	0	I	II	III

THEME 3 SECTION 9:   Nutrition and Digestion
Exercise 5.9   Technology – Which washing-up liquid? – *Experimental design 3*

Skills indicated by * need to be assessed during the course of the Exercise.

Skill area – Experimental design 3

All skills within the skill area *Experimental design* (with the exception of the skill *Recording*) are marked using the following rating scale:

Criteria	Mark	Competency Level
Skill accomplished with no assistance	9–7	III
Skill accomplished with occasional assistance	6–4	II
Skill accomplished with regular assistance	3–1	I
Incapable of accomplishing skill	0	0

Skill – Problem identification/hypothesis formulation

General criterion: Can identify a problem/formulate a hypothesis.

Specific criteria for this Exercise:

1.

Criteria	Competency Level
Increases the surface area of the fat by breaking it down into small globules.	III
Breaks the fat down/into small globules.	I and II

2. Does 'Whizzo' break down the fat into smaller globules/ increase the surface area of the fat better than 'Superclean'?

3. Fat treated with 'Whizzo' has a greater surface area.

Skill – Apparatus selection

General criterion: Can select appropriate apparatus.

Specific criteria for this Exercise:

Apparatus	Materials/Reagents
Test tubes	Sample of 'Whizzo'
Bungs	Sample of 'Superclean'
Test tube rack	Sample of cooking oil
10 cm^3 measuring cylinder	
Dropping pipette	

Skill – Planning

General criterion: Can produce a logical, staged plan of an experiment with, where appropriate, controls.

Specific criteria for this Exercise:

1. Using the measuring cylinder, pour 2 cm^3 cooking oil into each of the test tubes A and B.

2. Using the dropping pipette, add 8 drops of 'Whizzo' to test tube A. Shake.

3. Clean the pipette. Add 8 drops of 'Superclean' to test tube B. Shake.

4. Observe both tubes after a stated period of time.

To obtain the highest level of competency (Level III) for this skill there must be an appreciation of replication (i.e. sets of test tubes A and B).

Skill – Procedure*

Criterion: Experimental plan followed competently and safely.

Skill – Recording

General criteria: What is recorded depends upon how sophisticated is the comparison of the observed results:

1. The readings can be in a simple table, recording the relative opaqueness of the contents of each test tube/set of test tubes using the naked eye.

2. A more refined method would be to shine a beam of light through the contents of each test tube and record the amount of light transmitted using a light meter. (Practically, this could be done by putting the contents of each tube into a slide projector cell – a flat-sided, transparent, plastic container – and shining the projector light through it in a darkened room.)

Specific criteria for this Exercise:

Results table

Test	Contents of tube	
	A	**B**
Visual comparison	(dense)	(less dense)

Criteria	Mark
Vertical columns headed	1
Horizontal column headed	1
Results recorded for both samples	1
Results recorded in *single* table	1
Overall layout clear	2

Maximum Competency Level = II

Mark Obtained	0	1 2 3	4 5 6
Competency Level	0	I	II

Skill – Interpretation

General criterion: Can reach appropriate conclusions/identify patterns.

Specific criteria for this Exercise: The more opaque the contents of the test tube, then the greater is the surface area of fat.

Hypothesis confirmed or, if rejected, a new hypothesis formulated.

Skill – Evaluation

General criterion: Can recognise 1. limitations of method;
2. method improvement;
3. areas of future study.

Specific criteria for this Exercise:

1. This will relate to (a) how simple/complicated the plan was, and (b) the candidates appreciation of (a).

2. Possibly finding an easier/more sophisticated method of comparison.

3. Comparing a range of washing-up liquids and producing a 'league table'.

THEME 3 SECTION 5:   Nutrition and Digestion

Exercise 5.10a   Investigating the enzyme catalase

Skills indicated by * need to be assessed during the course of the Exercise.

Skill area – Following instructions *

Criteria	Mark	Competency Level
Instructions followed *without assistance.* Procedure carried out *competently* and *safely.*	9–7	III
Instructions followed and procedures carried out with *occasional assistance.* Shows *awareness* of safety precautions but *sometimes careless.*	6–4	II
Instructions followed and procedures carried out only with *regular/constant supervision.* Uses safety precautions *only when reminded.*	3–1	I
Incapable of following instructions and carrying out procedures, or skill *not attempted*	0	0

Skill area – Measurement *

Criteria	Competency Level
All 6 volumes accurate to $\pm$ 0.1 cm^3	III
5 volumes accurate to $\pm$ 0.1 cm^3	II
4 volumes accurate to $\pm$ 0.1 cm^3	I
Less than 4 volumes accurate to $\pm$ 0.1 cm^3	0

Skill area – Recording

Results table

Biological material		Observation	Test with glowing splint
Potato	unboiled	effervescence*	relit
	boiled	no effervescence	did not relight
Liver	unboiled	strong effervescence	relit
	boiled	no effervescence	did not relight
Yeast	unboiled	strong effervescence	relit
	boiled	no effervescence	did nor relight

* or words to that effect

Criteria	Mark
Vertical columns headed	1
Horizontal columns headed	1
Unboiled/boiled material collated together	1
Full set of results recorded	1
No anomalous results/anomalous results noted and eliminated	1
Observation worded effectively	1
Results recorded in *single* table	1
Overall layout clear	2

Mark Obtained	0	1 2 3	4 5 6	7 8 9
Competency Level	0	I	II	III

THEME 3 SECTION 5: Nutrition and Digestion

Exercise 5.10b Interpreting the results of Exercise 5.10a

Skills indicated by * need to be assessed during the course of the Exercise.

Skill area – Interpretation

Question	Criteria	Mark
1.(a)	All unboiled material	1
(b)	Oxygen	1
(c)	Hydrogen peroxide	1
(d)	Catalase	1
(e)	Catalase denatured	1
2.	$2H_2O_2 ----\gg 2H_2O + O_2$	1
3. (a)	Equal masses of material	1
(b)	Either (i) measure (ruler) the maximum height the froth reached for each material, or (ii) use a measuring cylinder (20 cm^3) to measure volume of froth produced by each material	2

Mark Obtained	0	1 2 3	4 5 6	7 8 9
Competency Level	0	I	II	III

THEME 3 SECTION 5: Nutrition and Digestion

Exercise 5.11a & b Comparing how much Vitamin C there is in different fruit juices – *Experimental design*

Skills indicated by * need to be assessed during the course of the Exercise.

Skill area – Experimental design 1 and 2

All skills within the skill area *Experimental design* (with the exception of the skill *Recording*) are marked using the following rating scale:

Criteria	Mark	Competency Level
Skill accomplished with no assistance	9–7	III
Skill accomplished with occasional assistance	6–4	II
Skill accomplished with regular assistance	3–1	I
Incapable of accomplishing skill	0	0

Skill – Apparatus selection

General criterion: Can select appropriate apparatus

Specific criteria for this Exercise:

Additional apparatus required: 5 test tubes
Test tube rack
10 cm^3 measuring cylinder
1 dropping pipette

Skill – Planning

General criterion: Can produce a logical, staged plan of an experiment with, where appropriate, controls.

Specific criteria for this Exercise:

1. Pour 5 cm^3 DCPIP into the measuring cylinder.
2. Transfer to clean test tube.
3. Fill dropping pipette three quarters full with fruit juice A.
4. Add fruit juice A to DCPIP a drop at a time, shaking gently, until blue colour just disappears.
5. Record number of drops used. Wash out dropping pipette.
6. Repeat 1. to 5. for fruit juices B, C, D and E.

Skill – Procedure*

General criterion: Can follow an experimental plan competently and safely.

Specific criterion for this Exercise: Plan followed competently and safely.

Skill – Recording

Specific criteria for this Section:

1. *Results table*

Fruit juice	Number of drops of juice required to decolourise DCPIP
A B C D E	

Criteria	Mark
Vertical columns headed	1
Horizontal columns headed	1
Full set of results recorded	1
Results recorded in *single* table	1
Overall layout clear	2

Maximum Competency Level = II

Mark Obtained	0	1 2 3	4 5 6
Competency Level	0	I	II

2. *Graph*

Criteria	Mark
Sensible scale	1
Time on x axis	1
x axis labelled time (+ units)	2
y axis labelled Vitamin C content (+ units)	2
Points plotted accurately*	1
Points joined accurately*	1
Graph given a suitable title	1

*A mark must be obtained for each of these criteria for Competency Level III.

Mark Obtained	0	1 2 3	4 5 6	7 8 9
Competency Level	0	I	II	III

Questions 1, 2, 3 and 4(b) are not for assessment.

THEME 3 SECTION 5: Nutrition and Digestion
Exercise 5.12 Investigating how much energy a peanut contains

Skills indicated by * need to be assessed during the course of the Exercise.

Skill area – Following instructions*

Criteria	Mark	Competency Level
Instructions followed *without assistance*. Procedures carried out *competently* and *safely*.	9–7	III
Instructions followed and procedures carried out with *occasional assistance*. Shows *awareness* of safety precautions but *sometimes careless*.	6–4	II
Instructions followed and procedures carried out only with *regular/constant supervision*. Uses safety precautions *only when reminded*.	3–1	I
Incapable of following instructions and carrying out procedures, *or* skill *not attempted*	0	0

Skill area – Measurement*

Criteria	Competency Level
Temperature measured to within ± 1°C	III
Temperature measurement outside ± 1°C	0
Mass of peanut measured to within ± 0.1g	III
Mass of peanut measurement outside ± 0.1g	0

Skill area – Interpretation

In (a) Figures transposed correctly from results table. Multiplication correct.

(b) Maths correct. Decimal point in correct place.

(c) Energy produced by 1 g of peanuts $= \dfrac{1.0}{\text{mass of peanut}} \times$ energy produced by peanut.

Criteria	Competency Level
(a), (b) and (c) accomplished without assistance	III
(a) and (b) accomplished without assistance (c) accomplished with occasional assistance	II
(a) and (b) accomplished with occasional assistance (c) accomplished with considerable assistance	I
(a) and (b) accomplished with considerable assistance (c) not attempted, unable to be accomplished	0

THEME 3 SECTION 5:   Nutrition and Digestion

Exercise 5.13   The biscuit problem – *Experimental design 3*

Skills indicated by * need to be assessed during the course of the Exercise.

Skill area – Experimental design 3

All skills within the skill area *Experimental design* (with the exception of the skill *Recording*) are marked using the following rating scale:

Criteria	Mark	Competency Level
Skill accomplished with no assistance	9–7	III
Skill accomplished with occasional assistance	6–4	II
Skill accomplished with regular assistance	3–1	I
Incapable of accomplishing skill	0	0

Skill – Problem identification/hypothesis formulation

General criterion: Can identify a problem/formulate a hypothesis.

Specific criteria for this Exercise:

1. Per mass, the biscuit has a lower energy value.

2. Which biscuit has the lowest/highest energy value?

3. 'Slimmo' biscuits are less fattening because they have a lower energy value than 'Dietex' biscuits. (3. can be phrased 4 different ways.)

Skill – Apparatus selection

General criterion: Can select appropriate apparatus.

Specific criteria for this Exercise:

Apparatus required: Balance (weighing to 1 or 2 decimal places)   Boiling tube
Measuring cylinder (100 cm^3)   Stand, boss, clamp
°C thermometer   Bunsen burner

Skill – Planning

General criterion: Can produce a logical, staged plan of an experiment with, where appropriate, controls.

Specific criteria for this Exercise:

1. Dry the 2 biscuit samples (oven) to remove water (if necessary).
2. Set up boiling tube on stand using boss and clamp.
3. Add measured volume of water to boiling tube.
4. Take and record temperature of water.
5. Weigh and record a small mass of one of the biscuits.
6. Ignite biscuit sample, burning under water in boiling tube. Stirring.
7. Take and record temperature of water when burning ceases.
8. Repeat 2–7 for second biscuit. Indication given to need for experimental replication.

Skill – Procedure*

Specific criterion for this exercise: Plan (above) followed competently and safely.

Skill – Recording

Specific criteria for this Exercise:

Measurement	Slimmo	Dietex
Mass (g)		
Temperature of cold water (°C)		
Temp. of water after heating (°C)		
Rise in temperature (°C)		

Criteria	Mark
Vertical columns headed	1
Horizontal columns headed	1
Units of mass (g) stated	1
Units of temperature (°C) stated	1
Full set of results recorded	1
Temperature rise recorded	1
Results recorded in *single* table	1
Overall layout clear	2

Mark Obtained	0	1 2 3	4 5 6	7 8 9
Competency Level	0	I	II	III

Skill – Interpretation

General criterion: Can reach appropriate conclusions and identify patterns.

Specific criteria for this Exercise: If the mass of the two biscuits was the same, then the difference between the rises in temperature gives a direct comparison of the energy value of the biscuits. If not, procedures (a), (b) and (c) of Exercise 5.12 need to be followed to evaluate, in each case, the energy content of 1 g of biscuit.

Hypothesis confirmed or, if rejected, a new hypothesis formulated.

Skill – Evaluation

General criteria: Can recognise limitations of method/method improvement/area of future study.

Specific criteria for this Exercise: Limitations of method, e.g. uncontrolled heat losses/ temperature rise differences too small for accurate comparison.

Future study: Comparison of energy value of staple diet foods around the world, e.g. rice, bread, pasta, etc.

THEME 3 SECTION 5:   Nutrition and Digestion

Exercise 5.14a   Biotechnology – Investigating the action of a biological washing powder

Skills indicated by * need to be assessed during the course of the Exercise.

*Skill area – Following instructions**

Criteria	Mark	Competency Level
Instructions followed *without assistance*. Procedures carried out *competently* and *safely*.	9–7	III
Instructions followed and procedures carried out with *occasional assistance*. Shows *awareness* of safety precautions but *sometimes careless*.	6–4	II
Instructions followed and procedures carried out only with *regular/constant supervision*. Uses safety precautions *only when reminded*.	3–1	I
Incapable of following instructions and carrying out procedures, *or* skill *not attempted*	0	0

Skill area – Recording

Criteria	Mark
3 temperatures recorded	1
Temperature unit recorded (°C)	1
3 descriptions of material recorded	1
Descriptions recorded accurately	2
Presence/absence of oil recorded	1

Maximum Competency Level = II

Mark Obtained	0	1 2 3	4 5 6
Competency Level	0	I	II

THEME 3 SECTION 5:   Nutrition and Digestion

Exercise 5.14b   Interpreting the results of Exercise 5.14a

Skills indicated by * need to be assessed during the course of the Exercise.

Skill area – Interpretation

Question	Criteria	Mark
1.	Same material Same degree of staining for each material Same area of material Same volume of water Treatment for same length of time } $\frac{1}{2}$ mark each, maximum 2 marks	2
2. (a) (b)	Allows washing powder to contact material more efficiently Boiling action provides necessary agitation	1 1
3.	Control	1
4. (a) (b) (c)	Made soluble/converted to fatty acids and glycerol Enzyme/lipase Optimum temperature for enzyme activity	1 1 1
5.	More economical on electricity	1

Mark Obtained	0	1 2 3	4 5 6	7 8 9
Competency Level	0	I	II	III

Continued

THEME 3 SECTION 6:   Photosynthesis

Exercise 6.1   Testing a leaf for the presence of starch

Skills indicated by * need to be assessed during the course of the Exercise.

Skill area – Following instructons*

Criteria	Mark	Competency Level
Instructions followed *without assistance*. Procedures carried out *competently* and *safely*.	9–7	III
Instructions followed and procedures carried out with *occasional assistance*. Shows *awareness* of safety precautions but *sometimes careless*.	6–4	II
Instructions followed and procedures carried out only with *regular/ constant supervision*. Uses safety precautions *only when reminded*.	3–1	I
Incapable of following instructions and carrying out procedures, *or* skill *not attempted*.	0	0

THEME 3 SECTION 6:   Photosynthesis

Exercise 6.2a   Investigating whether chlorophyll is necessary for starch formation during photosynthesis

Skills indicated by * need to be assessed during the course of the Exercise.

Skill area – Manipulation*

Criteria	Mark
Water *boiled* prior to leaf immersion	1
Forceps used at all stages of leaf transfer	1
Bunsen burner turned *off* after leaf is 'fixed'	2
Leaf *fully* immersed in ethanol	1
Leaf *fully* decolourised by ethanol	1
Leaf *washed* prior to testing with iodine solution	1
Leaf placed *uppermost* in petri dish base	1
Leaf *flattened* on to base of petri dish	1

Mark Obtained	0	1 2 3	4 5 6	7 8 9
Competency Level	0	I	II	III

Skill area – Observation*

Criteria	Mark
Outline shape of both drawings the same, and identifiable from the leaf	1
Drawings of reasonable size in terms of space available	2
Chlorophyll/non-chlorophyll containing areas drawn accurately in A	1
Stained/non-stained areas drawn accurately in B	1
Areas on both drawings labelled, or indicated by colour or key	1
Drawing lines neat, clear, distinct.	2
Scale stated (e.g. × 1)	1

Mark Obtained	0	1 2 3	4 5 6	7 8 9
Competency Level	0	I	II	III

THEME 3 SECTION 6: Photosynthesis

Exercise 6.2b Interpreting the results of Exercise 6.2a

Skills indicated by * need to be assessed during the course of the Exercise.

Skill area – Interpretation

Question	Criteria	Mark
1. (a)	The green areas contain starch/the non-green areas do not contain starch.	1
(b)	Starch is formed only in the presence of chlorophyll/not formed in the absence of chlorophyll.	1
2.	The chlorophyll in the leaf.	2
3.	To make a record of the areas of the leaf prior to decolourising and treatment with iodine solution (1) so that an accurate comparison of chlorophyll-containing/starch-producing areas can be made (1).	2
4.	Decolourisation involves boiling ethanol which is inflammable.	1
5.	Non-green areas are non-living, *or* non-green areas synthesise nutrients *other than* starch, *or* all areas of the leaf photosynthesise but only the green areas produce starch, *or* any other sensible suggestion.	2

Mark Obtained	0	1 2 3	4 5 6	7 8 9
Competency Level	0	I	II	III

THEME 3 SECTION 6:   Photosynthesis

Exercise 6.3 Investigating whether carbon dioxide is necessary for starch formation during photosynthesis

Skills indicated by * need to be assessed during the course of the Exercise.

Skill area – Manipulation*

Criteria	Mark
Water *boiled* prior to leaf immersion	1
Forceps used at all stages of leaf transfer	1
Bunsen burner turned *off* after leaves are fixed	2
Leaves *fully* immersed in ethanol	1
Leaves *fully* decolourised by ethanol	1
Leaves *washed* prior to testing with iodine solution	1
Leaves placed *uppermost* in petri dish bases	1
Leaves *flattened* on to petri dish bases	1

Mark Obtained	0	1 2 3	4 5 6	7 8 9
Competency Level	0	I	II	III

THEME 3 SECTION 6:   Photosynthesis

Exercise 6.4 Investigating whether light is necessary for starch formation during photosynthesis

Skills indicated by * need to be assessed during the course of the Exercise.

*Skill area – Manipulation**

Criteria	Mark
Water *boiled* prior to leaf immersion	1
Forceps used at all stages of leaf transfer	1
Bunsen burner *turned off* after leaf is 'fixed'	2
Leaf *fully* immersed in ethanol	1
Leaf *fully* decolourised by ethanol	1
Leaf *washed* prior to testing with iodine solution	1
Leaf placed *uppermost* in petri dish base	1
Leaf *flattened* on to petri dish base	1

Mark Obtained	0	1 2 3	4 5 6	7 8 9
Competency Level	0	I	II	III

*Skill area – Observation**

Criteria	Mark
Outline of both drawings the same and identifiable from the leaf	1
Drawings of a reasonable size in terms of the space available	2
Stencil drawn accurately in A	1
Stained/unstained areas drawn accurately in B	1
Areas on both drawings labelled or indicated by colour or key	1
Drawing lines neat, clear, distinct	2
Scale stated (e.g. $\times$ 1)	1

Mark Obtained	0	1 2 3	4 5 6	7 8 9
Competency Level	0	I	II	III

THEME 3 SECTION 6:   Photosynthesis

Exercise 6.5a Investigating gas production by a green plant during photosynthesis

Skills indicated by * need to be assessed during the course of the Exercise.

Skill area – Following instructions*

Criteria	Mark	Competency Level
Instructions followed *without assistance*. Procedures carried out *competently and safely*.	9–7	III
Instructions followed and procedures carried out with *occasional assistance*. Shows *awareness* of safety precautions but *sometimes careless*.	6–4	II
Instructions followed and procedures carried out only with *regular/constant supervision*. Uses safety precautions *only when reminded*.	3–1	I
Incapable of following instructions and carrying out procedures *or* skill *not attempted*.	0	0

Skill area – Measurements*

Criteria	Competency Level
Volume measured within $\pm$ 0.1 cm^3	III
Volume measured outside $\pm$ 0.1 cm^3	0

Skill area – Recording

Criteria	Mark
9 results entered	1
No anomalous results/anomalous results noted and eliminated	1
Mean number entered	1
Mean recorded to nearest whole number	1
Distance expressed as cm	1
Number of gas bubbles evolved expressed as 'per min'	1

Maximum Competency Level = II

Mark Obtained	0	1	2	3	4	5	6
Competency Level	0		I			II	

THEME 3 SECTION 6:   Photosynthesis
Exercise 6.5b Interpreting the results of Exercise 6.5a

Skills indicated by * need to be assessed during the course of the Exercise.

Skill area – Interpretation

Question	Criteria	Mark
1.	To increase the carbon dioxide content of the water ($\frac{1}{2}$) and so maximise the rate of photosynthesis ($\frac{1}{2}$)	1
2.	To weigh down the pond weed	1
3. (a)	The higher/lower the light intensity the more/less gas is given off	1
(b)	Oxygen	1
(c)	Insert glowing splint into gas ($\frac{1}{2}$). Splint relights ($\frac{1}{2}$)	1
(d)	All bubbles are the same size/volume	1
4. (a)	Leaves	1
(b)	Pond weed with leaves removed (1) and treated according to Steps 1 to 6 of Exercise 6.5a (1)	2

Mark Obtained	0	1 2 3	4 5 6	7 8 9
Competency Level	0	I	II	III

THEME 3 SECTION 6:   Photosynthesis
Exercise 6.6 Which wavelength? – *Experimental design 2*

Skills indicated by * need to be assessed during the course of the Exercise.

Skill area – Experimental design 2

All skills within the skill area *Experimental design* (with the exception of the skill *Recording*) are marked using the following Rating Scale:

Criteria	Mark	Competency Level
Skill accomplished with no assistance	9–7	III
Skill accomplished with occasional assistance	6–4	II
Skill accomplished with regular assistance	3–1	I
Incapable of accomplishing skill	0	0

Skill – Apparatus selection

General criterion: Can select appropriate apparatus.

Specific criteria for this Exercise: As for Exercise 6.5a plus:

   (a) 6 coloured filters corresponding to the spectrum colours
   (b) A device for holding the filters in front of the lamp.

Skill – Planning

General criterion: Can produce a logical, staged plan of an experiment.

Specific criteria for this Exercise:

1. Set up weighted pond weed in measuring cylinder of carbon dioxide enriched water.

2. Set up lamp at *stated* distance from measuring cylinder.

3. Fix one of the filters in front of the lamp. Illuminate pond weed. Leave for 5 minutes, then count number of gas bubbles evolved in one minute. Record. Repeat on 2 more occasions. Obtain mean.

4. Repeat Step 3 for the 5 other filters, allowing conditions to establish each time before taking readings.

Skill – Procedure*

Specific criterion for this Exercise: Plan (above) followed competently and safely.

Skill – Recording

Colour of filters	Number of bubbles evolved (per min)			
	1	2	3	mean
Red				
Orange				
Yellow				
Green				
Blue				
Violet				

Criteria	Mark
Vertical columns headed	1
Horizontal columns headed	1
Bubbles evolved expressed as 'per min'	1
3 counts for each filter	1
Mean for counts recorded	1
Mean recorded to nearest whole number	1
Results recorded in *single* table	1
Overall layout clear	2

Mark Obtained	0	1 2 3	4 5 6	7 8 9
Competency Level	0	I	II	III

Skill – Interpretation

General criterion: Can reach appropriate conclusions and identify patterns.

Specific criteria for this Exercise:

1. Correct wavelength(s) selected in terms of *results obtained*.

2. Rate of evolution of gas bubbles is a measure of rate of photosynthesis. The colour(s) above, gave the highest rate of gas production and so were responsible for the highest rate of photosynthesis.

Skill – Evaluation

General criterion: Can recognise limitations of method/method improvement/areas of future study.

Specific criteria for this Exercise: Limitations of method (e.g. possibly overheating pondweed; filters of different colour *density*).

Future study: Commercial applications – illumination of indoor food crops (lettuce, tomatoes, celery) using only effective wavelengths of light to improve yield.

THEME 3 SECTION 6:   Photosynthesis

Exercise 6.7 Extracting chlorophyll from leaves and separating the chlorophyll into its pigments

Skills indicated by * need to be assessed during the course of the Exercise.

Skill area – Measurement*

Length (Step 1)

Criteria	Competency Level
Length of paper measured to within ± 0.1 cm	III
Length of paper measured outside ± 0.1 cm	0

Skill area – Manipulation*

Criteria	Mark
Leaves cut and ground thoroughly	2
Filter paper folded correctly	1
Level of extract below top of filter paper throughout filtration	1
Satisfactory volume of filtrate obtained	1
Spot of chlorophyll extract obtained in a high enough concentration	1

Completed set up has:
    bottom edge of paper dipped in solvent
    chlorophyll spot above solvent level
    paper clear of sides of boiling tube
	1
	1
	1

Mark Obtained	0	1 2 3	4 5 6	7 8 9
Competency Level	0	I	II	III

Skill area – Observation*

Criteria	Mark
Chromatography paper drawn full size	1
Sequence of pigments from pencil line:	
1st green	1
2nd blue/green	1
3rd yellow/brown	1
4th yellow	1
Distance of pigments from spot on pencil line*	
green 2.7 cm	1
blue/green 4.0 cm	1
yellow/brown 4.3 cm	1
yellow 5.7 cm	1

*This assumes that the distance between the chlorophyll extract spot and solvent front at the end of the Exercise is 9 cm. It is *not* anticipated that pupils will obtain such accuracy. However, to obtain the mark there must be evidence that the distance of pigment from the spot has been *measured*.

Mark Obtained	0	1 2 3	4 5 6	7 8 9
Competency Level	0	I	II	III

THEME 3 SECTION 6:   Photosynthesis

Exercise 6.8 The leaf colour problem – *Experimental design 3*

Skills indicated by * need to be assessed during the course of the Exercise.

Skill area – Experimental design

All skills within the skill area *Experimental design* (with the exception of the skill *Recording*) are marked using the following rating scale:

Criteria	Mark	Competency Level
Skill accomplished with no assistance	9–7	III
Skill accomplished with occasional assistance	6–4	II
Skill accomplished with regular assistance	3–1	I
Incapable of accomplishing skill	0	0

Skill – Problem identification/hypothesis formulation

General criterion: Can identify a problem/formulate a hypothesis.

Specific criteria for this Exercise:

1. Do plants, which do not have green leaves, photosynthesise?

2. (a) Chlorophyll
   (b) No

3. Separate pigments of leaf extract by chromatography to see if colour and position of pigments obtained are the same as that for chlorophyll.

4. Beech leaves can photosynthesise because chlorophyll is present, (or, beech leaves cannot photosynthesise because chlorophyll is not present).

Skill – Apparatus selection

General criterion: Can select appropriate apparatus.

Specific criterion for this Exercise: Apparatus/reagents as for Exercise 6.7; materials – beech leaves.

Skill – Planning

General criterion: Can produce a logical, staged plan of an experiment with, where appropriate, controls.

Specific criteria for this Exercise: Steps 1 to 10 of Exerise 6.7, using beech leaf extract. (A control would be running a parallel experiment using green leaves (e.g. geranium). However, these results have already been obtained in Exercise 6.7 and so a control is not really necessary.)

Skill – Procedure*

Specific criterion for this Exercise: Plan (above) followed competently and safely.

Skill – Recording

If unsatisfactory results were obtained for Exercise 6.7, the pupil should be given details of pigment separation for a green leaf (See Exercise 6.7 Mark Scheme – *Observation*, page 128).

Specific criteria for this Exercise:

Pigment colour	Distance moved from pencil line (cm)	
	Green leaf*	Beech leaf
Green		
Blue/Green		
Yellow/Brown		
Yellow		
Others		

*from Exercise 6.7

Criteria	Mark
Vertical columns headed	1
Horizontal columns headed	1
Unit of distance (cm) stated	1
Distances recorded to 1 decimal place	1
Minimum of three pigments recorded	2
Results recorded in *single* table	1
Overall layout clear	2

Mark Obtained	0	1 2 3	4 5 6	7 8 9
Competency Level	0	I	II	III

a beech leaf.

Skill – Interpretation

General criterion: Can reach appropriate conclusions and identify patterns.

Specific criteria for this Exercise: Accuracy of comparison will depend upon the relative distances travelled by the two solvent fronts. In general terms, however, there should be appreciation of the similarity of the pigments in a green leaf and a beech leaf.

Hypothesis confirmed or, if rejected, a new hypothesis formulated.

Skill – Evaluation

General criterion: Can recognise limitations of method/method improvement.

Specific criteria for this Exercise: See above with reference to relative distances travelled by the two solvent fronts.

THEME 3 SECTION 6:   Photosynthesis

Exercise 6.9a Investigating the action of potato juice on glucose

Skills indicated by * need to be assessed during the course of the Exercise.

Skill area – Manipulation*

Criteria	Mark
Potato ground to a watery paste	2
Filter paper folded correctly	1
Level of extract *below* top of filter paper throughout filtration	1
Satisfactory volume of filtrate obtained	1
Dropping pipette washed out (Steps 5 and 6)	1
Spotting tile contents mixed (Step 6)	1
No surplus solution on spotting tile surface	1
Iodine solution added at 2 minute intervals	1

Mark Obtained	0	1 2 3	4 5 6	7 8 9
Competency Level	0	I	II	III

Skill area – Measurement*

Criteria	Competency Level
Time recorded within ± 1 second	III
Time recorded outside ± 1 second	0

THEME 3 SECTION 6: Photosynthesis
Exercise 6.9b Interpreting the results of Exercise 6.9a

Skills indicated by * need to be assessed during the course of the Exercise.

Skill area – Interpretation

Question	Criteria	Mark
1.	No	1
2.	Starch grains are retained on the filter paper	1
3.	Enzyme/carbohydrase/amylase	1
4.	Boil half the sample of potato juice to denature any enzyme present (1). Repeat Steps 4 to 9 for the boiled sample (1)	2
5.	Enzyme activity starts *immediately* the potato juice is added (1). Whether the iodine solution is added at time 0 or time 12 mins, the conversion of glucose phosphate to starch will take the same length of time (1)	2
6.	Glucose is soluble. Starch is insoluble (1). Carbohydrates can be stored only in an insoluble form (i.e. starch is not mobile) (1)	2

Mark Obtained	0	1	2	3	4	5	6	7	8	9
Competency Level	0		I			II			III	

Continued

THEME 3 SECTION 7:   Water Relations in Plants

Exercise 7.1a   Investigating the effects of tap water and salt water on the mass of potato discs

Skills indicated by * need to be assessed during the course of the Exercise.

Skill area – Following instructions*

Criteria	Mark	Competency Level
Instructions 2. to 9. followed *without assistance*. Procedures carried out *competently* and *safely*.	9–7	III
Instructions 2. to 9. followed and procedures carried out with *occasional assistance*. Shows *awareness* of safety precautions but *sometimes careless*.	6–4	II
Instructions 2. to 9. followed, and procedures carried out only with *regular/constant supervision*. Uses safety precautions *only when reminded*.	3–1	I
Incapable of following instructions 2. to 9. and carrying out procedures *or* skill *not attempted*.	0	0

Skill area – Manipulation*

Measurement of disc thickness (random sample of 5 discs)

Criteria	Competency Level
All disc measurements accurate to ± 5.0 mm thick	III
4 disc measurements accurate to ± 5.0 mm thick	II
3 disc measurements accurate to ± 5.0 mm thick	I
Less than 3 disc measurements accurate to ± 5.0 mm thick	0

Skill area – Measurement*

Criteria	Competency Level
All 4 weighings of discs accurate to ± 0.1 g	III
3 weighings of discs accurate to ± 0.1 g	II
2 weighings of discs accurate to ± 0.1 g	I
Less than 2 weighings accurate to ± 0.1 g	0

Skill area – Recording

Criteria	Mark
4 results recorded	1
Results recorded to 1 decimal place	1
Change in mass recorded to 1 decimal place	1
Mass and change in mass expressed as g	1
Mass and change in mass expressed as + or − g	2

Maximum Competency Level = II

Mark Obtained	0	1 2 3	4 5 6
Competency Level	0	I	II

THEME 3 SECTION 7: Water Relations in Plants

Exercise 7.1b Interpreting the results of Exercise 7.1a

Skills indicated by * need to be assessed during the course of the Exercise.

Skill area – Interpretation 1

Question 1

Criteria	Competency Level
Calculations accomplished without assistance	III
Calculations accomplished with limited assistance	II
Calculations accomplished with considerable assistance	I
Calculations not attempted	0

Skill area – Interpretation 2

Questions 2 and 3

Questions	Criteria	Mark
2. (a) (b)	Those in tap water ($\frac{1}{2}$) Those in salt water ($\frac{1}{2}$)	1
(c)	Water entering/leaving discs	2
3.	Clear explanation of osmosis	4
	General reference to discs	1
	Specific reference to membranes and sap of potato disc cells	1

Mark Obtained	0	1 2 3	4 5 6	7 8 9
Competency Level	0	I	II	III

THEME 3 SECTION 7:   Water Relations in Plants

Exercise 7.2   Which salt solution? – *Experimental design 2*

Skills indicated by * need to be assessed during the course of the Exercise.

Skill area – Experimental design 2

All skills within the skill area *Experimental design* (with the exception of the skill *Recording*) are marked using the following rating scale:

Criteria	Mark	Competency Level
Skill accomplished with no assistance	9–7	III
Skill accomplished with occasional assistance	6–4	II
Skill accomplished with regular assistance	3–1	I
Incapable of accomplishing skill	0	0

Skill – Apparatus selection

General criterion: Can select appropriate apparatus.

Specific criteria for this Exercise:

Apparatus required: White tile   Filter papers
                Scalpel   Direct-reading balance (to 1 decimal place)
                Section lifter   Cork borer (15–20 mm diameter)
                Ruler
Biological material: 1 large potato

Skill – Planning

General criterion Can produce a logical, staged plan of an experiment.
Specific criteria for this Exercise:

1. Using the cork borer, remove cylinders of tissue from potato.

2. Cut the cylinders into discs of equal thickness (e.g. 5.0 mm)

3. Divide the discs into 3 batches.

4. Blot dry each batch.

5. Weigh each batch (to 0.1 g). Record masses in results table.

6. Put one batch into each of the salt solutions A, B, and C.

7. Leave for 20 minutes. Remove (using the section lifter). Blot dry and reweigh. Record masses in results table.

Skill – Procedure*

Specific criterion for this Exercise: Plan (above) followed competently and safely.

Skill – Recording

Solution	Mass of discs (g)		Change in mass (g)	Change in mass (%)
	Before immersing in solution	After immersing in solution		
A B C				

Criteria	Mark
Vertical columns headed	1
Horizontal columns headed	1
Units of mass (g) stated	1
Full set of results recorded	1
% change in mass tabulated	1
% change in mass recorded	1
Results recorded in *single* table	1
Overall layout clear	2

Mark Obtained	0	1 2 3	4 5 6	7 8 9
Competency Level	0	I	II	III

Skill – Interpretation

General criterion: Can reach appropriate conclusions and identify patterns.

Specific criteria for this Exercise:

1. Correct solution selected (i.e. the solution which produced the greatest % change in mass of the discs).

2. The more concentrated the solution is, the more water will leave the discs (osmotic effect) and thus the greater will be their percentage decrease in mass.

Skill – Evaluation

General criterion: Can recognise limitations of methods/method improvement.

Specific criteria for this Exercise: If there was sufficient difference between the concentrations of A, B, and C, (see page 000) the results should be clear-cut. However, possible suggestions could be: use larger cork borer; cut thinner discs (to increase surface area and optimise the osmotic effect); Stir solutions to increase osmotic gradient; Record mass to 2 decimal places.

THEME 3 SECTION 7:   Water Relations in Plants

Exercise 7.3 Investigating the passage of water through the stem of a plant

Skills indicated by * need to be assessed during the course of the Exercise.

Skill area – Manipulation*

1. Dissection

Step	Criteria	Mark
1.	Section transverse not oblique	1
3.	Sensible use of instruments	2
	1 cm length (approx) dissected out	2
	Parenchyma removed completely (2) partially (1)	2
5.	Tissue squashed effectively and sensibly	2

Mark Obtained	0	1	2	3	4	5	6	7	8	9
Competency Level	0		I			II			III	

2. Microscope adjustment

Criteria	Mark
Mirror adjusted for optimum clarity	3
Condenser adjusted for optimum clarity	3
Microscope focused for optimum clarity	3

Mark Obtained	0	1	2	3	4	5	6	7	8	9
Competency Level	0		I			II			III	

*Skill area – Observation**

1. Drawing of gross structure (Step 2)

Criteria	Mark
Drawing identifiable from section	2
Drawing of reasonable size in terms of space available	2
Drawing of stained regions in proportion to rest of tissue (1) Stained regions clearly indicated (1)	2
Drawing lines neat, clear, distinct	2
Scale stated (e.g. $\times 2$)	1

Mark Obtained	0	1 2 3	4 5 6	7 8 9
Competency Level	0	I	II	III

2. Drawing of fine detail (Step 7)

Criteria	Mark
Drawing identifiable from slide	2
Drawing of reasonable size in terms of space available	2
Spiral shown as a double line (not single line)	2
Drawing lines neat, clear, distinct	2
Scale stated (e.g. $\times 200$)	1

Mark Obtained	0	1 2 3	4 5 6	7 8 9
Competency Level	0	I	II	III

THEME 3 SECTION 7:   Water Relations in Plants

Exercise 7.4a   Investigating water uptake in the shoot of a plant

Skills indicated by * need to be assessed during the course of the Exercise.

Skill area – Following instructions*

Criteria	Mark	Competency Level
Instructions followed *without assistance*. Procedures carried out *competently* and *safely*.	9–7	III
Instructions followed and procedures carried out with *occasional assistance*. Shows *awareness* of safety precautions but *sometimes careless*.	6–4	II
Instructions followed and procedures carried out only with *regular/ constant supervision*. Uses safety precautions *only when reminded*.	3–1	I
Incapable of following instructions and carrying out procedures *or* skill *not attempted*.	0	0

Skill area – Measurement*

1. Volume

Criteria	Competency Level
Both volume measurements accurate to $\pm$ 0.1 cm^3	III
One volume measurement accurate to $\pm$ 0.1 cm^3	II

2. Mass

Criteria	Competency Level
Both mass measurements accurate to $\pm$ 0.1 g	III
One mass measurement accurate to $\pm$ 0.1 g	II

THEME 3 SECTION 7: Water Relations in Plants
Exercise 7.4b Interpreting the results of Exercise 7.4a

Skills indicated by * need to be assessed during the course of the Exercise.

Skill area – Interpretation

(NB Figures given have been derived from the printed table in Exercise 7.4b)

Question	Criteria	Mark
1.	To prevent air entering cut end of shoot	1
2.	To prevent loss of water by evaporation from water surface	1
3. (a)	3.4 g	1
(b)	0.3 g	1
4.	3.1 g	1
5.	Maintains turgidity (1). Required in chemical reactions (1) (e.g. photosynthesis)	2
6.	Break down of carbohydrates to produce energy (c.f. Exercise 5.11)/Senescence	2

Mark Obtained	0	1 2 3	4 5 6	7 8 9
Competency Level	0	I	II	III

Continued

THEME 3 SECTION 7:   Water Relations in Plants

Exercise 7.5a Investigating loss of water from the upper and lower surfaces of a privet leaf

Skills indicated by * need to be assessed during the course of the Exercise.

Skill area – Manipulation*

Criteria	Mark
Sticky tape cut to correct size	1
Sensible, temporary attachment of sticky tape to tile	1
Bunsen flame low, blue	1
Sensible drying of cobalt chloride paper	2
Cobalt chloride paper attached: 1. centrally to sticky tape 2. using forceps only	1 1
Sticky tape on leaf lamina and not over midrib	1
Stop clock started immediately after attachment	1

Mark Obtained	0	1	2	3	4	5	6	7	8	9
Competency Level	0		I			II			III	

Skill area – Measurement*

1. Length (4 measurements)

Criteria	Competency Level
Length of sides of cobalt chloride paper within ± 0.1 cm of 0.5 cm	III
3 measurements within ± 0.1 cm	II
2 measurements within ± 0.1 cm	I
Less than 2 measurements within ± 0.1 cm	0

2. Time

Criteria	Competency Level
Time recorded to ± 1 second	III
Time recorded outside ± 1 second	0

THEME 3 SECTION 7:   Water Relations in Plants
Exercise 7.5b Interpreting the results of Exercise 7.5a

Skills indicated by * need to be assessed during the course of the Exercise.

Skill area – Interpretation

Question	Criteria	Mark
1. (a)	Lower	1
(b)	Lower	1
(c)	Lower	1
2. (a)	To ensure seal is airtight over the cobalt chloride paper	1
(b)	To remove all traces of water that might have been absorbed from the air	1
(c)	To prevent moisture from fingers getting on to paper	1
(d)	Air-tight seal would be difficult to obtain	1
3.	No (unless area is larger than leaf surface/larger than sticky tape that attaches it)	1
4.	If the class has no prior knowledge of leaf structure (i.e. presence of stomata) any sensible suggestion should be credited (e.g. lower surface 'thinner' than upper surface)	1

Mark Obtained	0	1	2	3	4	5	6	7	8	9
Competency Level	0		I			II			III	

Continued

THEME 3 SECTION 7:   Water Relations in Plants

Exercise 7.6   Investigating the distribution of stomata on the upper and lower surfaces of a privet leaf

Skills indicated by * need to be assessed during the course of the Exercise.

Skill area – Manipulation*

1. Specimen preparation

Criteria	Mark
Satisfactory application of nail varnish	1
Nail varnish dry before removal attempted	1
Nail varnish removed cleanly with no attached epidermal tissue	2
Suitable area of nail varnish mounted	2
Cover slip placed using correct technique	1
No excess water on slide	1
No air bubbles	1

Mark Obtained	0	1 2 3	4 5 6	7 8 9
Competency Level	0	I	II	III

2. Microscope adjustment

Criteria	Mark
Mirror adjusted for optimum clarity	3
Condenser adjusted for optimum clarity	3
Microscope focused for optimum clarity	3

Mark Obtained	0	1 2 3	4 5 6	7 8 9
Competency Level	0	I	II	III

Skill area – Observation*

Criteria	Mark
Drawing identifiable from slide	2
Cells of reasonable size in terms of space available	2
Guard cells, stomata and epidermal cells labelled accurately on drawing of lower epidermis	1
Epidermal cells labelled on drawing of upper epidermis	1
Drawing lines neat, clear, distinct	2
Scale stated (e.g. × 400)	1

Mark Obtained	0	1	2	3	4	5	6	7	8	9
Competency Level	0		I			II			III	

THEME 3 SECTION 7:   Water Relations in Plants

Exercise 7.7   Estimating the number of stomata on the lower surface of a privet leaf

Skills indicated by * need to be assessed during the course of the Exercise.

Skill area – Manipulation*

1. Specimen preparation

Criteria	Mark
Satisfactory application of nail varnish	1
Nail varnish dry before removal attempted	1
Nail varnish removed cleanly with no attached epidermal tissue	2
Suitable area of nail varnish mounted	2
Cover slip placed using correct technique	1
No excess water on slide	1
No air bubbles	1

Mark Obtained	0	1	2	3	4	5	6	7	8	9
Competency Level	0		I			II			III	

2. Microscope adjustment

Criteria	Mark
Mirror adjusted for optimum clarity	3
Condenser adjusted for optimum clarity	3
Microscope focused for optimum clarity	3

Mark Obtained	0	1	2	3	4	5	6	7	8	9
Competency Level	0		I			II			III	

Skill area – Measurement*

1. Leaf area

Area of leaf	Competency Level
2% error	III
5% error	II
10% error	I

2. Stomatal count

Number of stomata in field of view	Competency Level
10% error	III
15% error	II
20% error	I

Select leaves with an area and shape which fall into the range indicated by the outlines below. This will ensure:

1. The number of stomata per unit area will be similar for all leaves.
2. The leaf area calculated by the pupil can be checked quickly by tracing the outlines below on to acetate sheet and using these as templates to fit over the pupil's own outline drawing of the leaf.

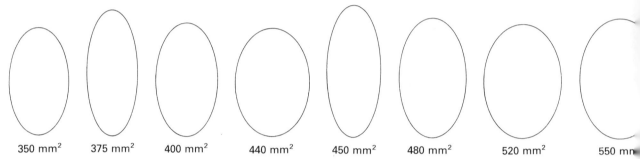

| 350 mm^2 | 375 mm^2 | 400 mm^2 | 440 mm^2 | 450 mm^2 | 480 mm^2 | 520 mm^2 | 550 mm |

Before the lesson, take a nail varnish impression of one of the leaves collected, to obtain a figure for number of stomata in the field of view ($\times$ 400). This should be in the region of 45.

Skill area – Interpretation

Calculation:

Stage 1: Number of stomata in an area of $0.18 \text{ mm}^2 = A$

Stage 2: Number of stomata in an area of $1.0 \text{ mm}^2 = \dfrac{0.1}{0.18} \times A$

Stage 3: Total area of lower leaf surface $= Y \text{ mm}^2$
Therefore, total number of stomata on lower leaf $= \dfrac{0.1}{0.18} \times A \times Y$

Criteria	Competency Level
Stages 1, 2, and 3 accomplished without assistance	III
Stages 1, 2, and 3 accomplished with limited assistance	II
Stages 1, 2, and 3 accomplished with considerable assistance	I
Calculation not attempted	0

THEME 3 SECTION 7:   Water Relations in Plants

Exercise 7.8   Investigating rate of water loss (transpiration) from the leaves of a shoot

Skills indicated by * need to be assessed during the course of the Exercise.

*Skill area – Manipulation**

Criteria	Mark
Cut end of shoot remains under water during Steps 1 and 2	1
Leaves remain above water during Steps 1 and 2	1
Shoot fixed efficiently to capillary tubing	1
Final set-up air-tight with no leaks	3
Stable set-up of apparatus using clamp	1
Bubble introduced efficiently into capillary tube	1
Bubble returned efficiently after each reading	1

Mark Obtained	0	1 2 3	4 5 6	7 8 9
Competency Level	0	I	II	III

Skill area – Recording

Criteria	Mark
Table 1: 3 times recorded	1
Mean recorded	1
Units of time(s) entered	1
Table 2: 3 times recorded	1
Mean recorded	1
Units of time(s) entered	1

Maximum Competency Level = II

Mark Obtained	0	1 2 3	4 5 6
Competency Level	0	I	II

THEME 3 SECTION 8:   Respiratory/Blood and Circulation

Exercise 8.1   Comparing the amount of carbon dioxide in inhaled and exhaled air

Skills indicated by * need to be assessed during the course of the Exercise.

Skill area – Manipulation*

Criteria	Mark
T-piece connected firmly (1) and safely (1) to pieces of glass tubing	2
4 pieces of glass tubing assembled correctly with reference to drawing	2
Limewater *above* levels of long arms of glass tubing (1) but *below* levels of short arms (1)	2
T-piece not facing downwards	1
Sensible use of apparatus to obtain results (Step 2), i.e. no limewater expelled from apparatus/sucked into mouth	2

Mark Obtained	0	1	2	3	4	5	6	7	8	9
Competency Level	0		I			II			III	

THEME 3 SECTION 8:   Respiration/Blood and Circulation

Exercise 8.2a   Investigating gas exchange in other organisms

Skills indicated by * need to be assessed during the course of the Exercise.

Skill area – Manipulation*

Criteria	Mark
Base of wire 'cage' about 0.5 cm above level of sodium hydroxide solution and *not* touching it	1
Short arm of capillary tube inserted into boiling tube	1
Organisms placed efficiently into boiling tube	2
Successful introduction of ink into capillary tubes (Steps 3 and 8)	1
Successful removal of ink from capillary tubes (Step 5b)	1
Ruler used for Steps 4 and 9	1
Boiling tubes not handled during Steps 2, 3, 4 and 7, 8, 9.	2

Mark Obtained	0	1	2	3	4	5	6	7	8	9
Competency Level	0		I			II			III	

THEME 3 SECTION 8: Respiration/Blood and Circulation

Exercise 8.2b Interpreting the results of Exercise 8.2a

Skills indicated by * need to be assessed during the course of the Exercise.

Skill area – Interpretation 1

Question	Criteria	Mark
1. (a)	Carbon dioxide and oxygen	1
(b)	Carbon dioxide	1
(c)	Oxygen	1
2. (a)	The oxygen used up by the organisms is not replaced by carbon dioxide (1). The air pressure in the boiling tube decreases (1). The air pressure outside the boiling tube is greater than that inside the boiling tube, so the ink drop is pushed towards the respiring organisms (1)	3
(b)	Poppet beads are non-living and so oxygen is not used up (1). The air pressure inside and outside the boiling tube remains constant (1)	2
3.	Wire cages allow for diffusion of carbon dioxide into sodium hydroxide solution	1

Mark Obtained	0	1 2 3	4 5 6	7 8 9
Competency Level	0	I	II	III

Skill area – Interpretation 2

Question	Criteria	Mark
1.	For a given volume of oxygen taken up by the organisms, the distance moved by the ink drop is greater in the capillary tube than it would be in ordinary glass tubing (1). It can thus be measured more accurately (1)	2
2.	There were more blowfly larvae (1)	2
	They were constantly moving (using up more energy and so requiring more oxygen) (1)	
3.	The organisms would have to have the same total mass	1
4.	Heat from the hands (1) caused the air in the boiling tubes to expand and push the drop of ink towards the open ends of the capillary tubes (1)	2
5. (a)	$0.2 \, cm^2 \times 3 \, cm = 0.6 \, cm^3$ (1)	2
(b)	$0.2 \, cm^2 \times 5 \, cm = 1.0 \, cm^3$ (1)	

Mark Obtained	0	1 2 3	4 5 6	7 8 9
Competency Level	0	I	II	III

THEME 3 SECTION 8:   Respiration/Blood and Circulation

Exercise 8.3a   Biotechnology – investigating the effect of yeast on a sugar solution in the absence of oxygen

Skills indicated by * need to be assessed during the course of the Exercise.

Skill area – Following instructions*

Criteria	Mark	Competency Level
Instructions followed *without assistance*. Procedures carried out *competently* and *safely*.	9–7	III
Instructions followed and procedures carried out with *occasional assistance*. Shows *awareness* of safety precautions but *sometimes careless*.	6–4	II
Instructions followed and procedures carried out only *with regular/constant supervision*. Uses safety precautions *only when reminded*.	3–1	I
Incapable of following instructions and carrying out procedures *or* skill *not attempted*.	0	0

Skill area – Measurement*

1. Volume

Criteria	Competency Level
Volume measured to ± 0.1 cm^3	III
Volume measured outside ± 0.1 cm^3	0

2. Temperature

Criteria	Competency Level
Both temperatures measured to ± 1°C	III
1 temperature measured to ± 1°C	II

THEME 3 SECTION 8:   Respiration/Blood and Circulation
Exercise 8.3b   Interpreting the results of Exercise 8.3a

Skills indicated by * need to be assessed during the course of the Exercise.

Skill area – Interpretation

Question	Criteria	Mark
1. (a)	Boiling removes dissolved oxygen in the sugar solution	1
(b)	Hot glucose solution would kill the yeast	1
2.	To prevent the entry of atmospheric oxygen into the sugar-yeast mixture	1
3.	Carbon dioxide and alcohol	2
4.	Yeast was respiring (1) and producing heat energy (1)	2
5.	Drawing/diagram as for that of Exercise 8.3a except for no yeast suspension/dead yeast suspension in the boiling tube	2

Mark Obtained	0	1 2 3	4 5 6	7 8 9
Competency Level	0	I	II	III

d according to instructions (Step 3)

THEME 3 SECTION 8:   Respiration/Blood and Circulation
Exercise 8.4a   Biotechnology – Investigating the effect of yeast on dough

Skills indicated by * need to be assessed during the course of the Exercise.

Skill area – Manipulation*

Criteria	Mark
Correct quantities of sugar and flour measured out (Step 1)	2
Water added according to instructions (Step 3)	2
Dough of acceptable constituency	1
Both beakers oiled as instructed (Step 4b)	1
Two portions of dough of equal size (Step 5)	1
Yeast added and mixed correctly (Step 6)	2

Mark Obtained	0	1 2 3	4 5 6	7 8 9
Competency Level	0	I	II	III

Skill area – Measurement*

Volume

Criteria	Competency Level
Volume measured to $\pm$ 0.1 cm^3	III
Volume measured outside $\pm$ 0.1 cm^3	0

Skill area – Observation*

Criteria		Mark
Dough with yeast	Dough without yeast	
Increase in volume/size	Volume/size has stayed the same	2
Dough expanded to cover bottom of beaker	Dough has stayed same shape	1
Gas/air bubbles in dough	No gas/air bubbles in dough	2
Surface 'skin' present	No surface 'skin'	1
Dough, beneath surface, is 'elastic'	Dough breaks up easily	2
Dough 'smells'	No obvious smell	1

Mark Obtained	0	1 2 3	4 5 6	7 8 9
Competency Level	0	I	II	III

THEME 3 SECTION 8:   Respiration/Blood and Circulation

Exercise 8.4b Interpreting the results of Exercise 8.4a

Skills indicated by * need to be assessed during the course of the Exercise.

Skill area – interpretation

Question	Criteria	Mark
1.	Carbon dioxide	1
2.	Respiration	1
3.	Sugar	1
4.	Yeast will respire more rapidly and produce more carbon dioxide (1), so the dough will rise more (1)	2
5.	So that an accurate comparison could be made	1
6.	So that the yeast cells were dispersed through/in contact with all the dough (1) and so could undergo cell respiration more efficiently (1)	2
7.	*Boiled* and cooled yeast plus dough (instead of dough without yeast)	1

Mark Obtained	0	1 2 3	4 5 6	7 8 9
Competency Level	0	I	II	III

THEME 3 SECTION 8:   Respiration/Blood and Circulation

Exercise 8.5 Biotechnology – The ideal loaf – *Experimental design 3*

Skills indicated by * need to be assessed during the course of the Exercise.

Skill area – Experimental design 3

All skills within the skill area *Experimental design* (with the exception of the skill *Recording*) are marked using the following rating scale:

Criteria	Mark	Competency Level
Skill accomplished with no assistance	9–7	III
Skill accomplished with occasional assistance	6–4	II
Skill accomplished with regular assistance	3–1	I
Incapable of accomplishing skill	0	0

Skill – Problem identification/hypothesis formulation

General criterion: Can identify a problem/formulate a hypothesis.

Specific criteria for this Exercise:

1. What is the optimum (best) temperature for the rising of dough?

2. Yeast

3. Carbon dioxide

4. The warmer it is, the more carbon dioxide is produced by the yeast (and the more the dough rises)

5. Yeast produces most carbon dioxide at a temperature of *

*The temperature must be stated. The stated temperature can be *any* temperature which can be attained and maintained *in the laboratory* (i.e. it would be expected that pupils would select a temperature between 0°C and 100°C).

Skill – Apparatus selection

General criterion: Can select appropriate apparatus.

Specific criteria for this Exercise:

Apparatus/material required: Test tube rack   Thermometer(s)
                               Test tubes   Yeast
                               Water bath(s)   20 cm³ measuring cylinder

Skill – Planning

General criterion: Can produce a logical, staged plan for an experiment. Because the experiment is investigating the optimum temperature for the evolution of the maximum volume of carbon dioxide by the yeast, the making of dough is not required.

Specific criteria for this Exercise:

1. Obtain a sample of fresh yeast/activated dried yeast.

2. Put equal volumes/masses of yeast into 3 test tubes.

3. Place one sample of yeast in a water bath maintained at:
   (a) 5°C *above* the temperature stated in the hypothesis;
   (b) the temperature stated in the hypothesis;
   (c) 5°C *below* the temperature stated in the hypothesis.

4. Observe the amount of frothing/evolution of carbon dioxide in the 3 test tubes after a stated period of time.

Notes:
Step 3 (above) is obviously a basic requirement, but availability of thermometers is going to limit the *number* of different temperatures at which experiments can be conducted. Extra credit should be given to pupils who appreciate that yeast samples should be maintained at temperature differences of, say, 5°C, for 20°C above and below the temperature stated in the hypothesis. For experiments involving widely separated temperatures (e.g. 20°C, 40°C, 100°C) the relative amount of frothing would be a satisfactory indication of the volumes of carbon dioxide produced. Extra credit should be given for suggesting a method of determining the relative rate of carbon dioxide production, e.g. by modifying the procedure in Exercise 8.3a and using hydrogen carbonate indicator to see which experiment caused the indicator to change colour the first, or by passing the carbon dioxide through glass tubing into a beaker of water and counting the gas bubbles evolved over a stated period of time.

Skill – Procedure*

Specific criteria for this Exercise: Plan (above) followed competently and safely.

Skill – Recording

Specific Criteria for this Exercise:

Temperature °C	Relative amount of frothing
e.g.	
40	little
45	much
50	none

Criteria	Mark
Vertical columns headed	1
Horizontal columns headed	1
Unit of temperature (°C) stated	1
Results recorded in a *single* table	1
Overall layout clear	2

Maximum Competency Level = II

Mark Obtained	0	1	2	3	4	5	6
Competency Level	0		I			II	

Skill – Interpretation

General Criterion: Can reach appropriate conclusions and identify patterns.

Specific criteria for this Exercise: Results interpreted correctly. Hypothesis confirmed or, if rejected, a new hypothesis formulated (i.e. on the evidence of the Exercise, sensibly changing the temperature stated in the hypothesis).

Skill – Evaluation

General criteria: Can recognise limitations of method/method improvement/ areas of future study.

Specific criteria for this Exercise: Limitations of method.

Future study: Optimum temperature of yeast for alcoholic fermentation.

THEME 3 SECTION 8:   Respiration/Blood and Circulation

Exercise 8.6 Investigating (a) the external features of a fish, and (b) gill structure

Skills indicated by * need to be assessed during the course of the Exercise.

Skill area – Observation 1*

Common features (Step 1)

Criteria	Mark

Both fish have:
    Mouth
    Eyes
    Scales
    Fins
	1
	1
	1
	1

Fin situated on the side of the body, behind the head	1
Streamlined shape	1

Contrasting features (Step 2)

Criteria		Mark
Lesser Sand Eel	**Whitebait**	
Larger/longer	Smaller/shorter	1
Fin on upper surface is $\frac{3}{4}$ length of body	Fin on upper surface small	1
Fin on lower surface is length of body	2 small fins on lower surface	1
Tail fin 'V'-shaped	Tail fin not 'V'-shaped	1
Lower lip sticks out prominently	Lower lip sticks out marginally	1

Maximum mark = 9.

Mark Obtained	0	1　2　3	4　5　6	7　8　9
Competency Level	0	I	II	III

Skill area – Observation 2*

Dissection drawing (Step 4)

Criteria	Mark
Drawing identifiable from dissection	2
Drawing of reasonable size in terms of space available	2
Some indication of gills being composed of filaments	2
Drawing lines neat, clear, distinct	2
Scale stated (e.g. × 2)	1

Mark Obtained	0	1 2 3	4 5 6	7 8 9
Competency Level	0	I	II	III

Skill area – Observation 3*

Drawing of fine detail (Step 7)

Criteria	Mark
Drawing identifiable from slide	2
Drawing of reasonable size in terms of space available	2
Lateral branches of gill filaments drawn	2
Drawing lines neat, clear, distinct	2
Scale stated (e.g. × 50)	1

Mark Obtained	0	1 2 3	4 5 6	7 8 9
Competency Level	0	I	II	III

Skill area – Manipulation 1*

Dissection (Step 3)

Criteria	Competency Level
Gill cover removed completely without assistance	III
Gill cover removed completely with occasional assistance	II
GIll cover removed completely with regular/constant assistance	I
Incapable of removing the gill cover/skill not attempted.	0

Skill area – Manipulation 2*

Microscope adjustment (Step 6)

Criteria	Mark
Mirror adjusted for optimum clarity	3
Condenser adjusted for optimum clarity	3
Mirror focused for optimum clarity	3

Mark Obtained	0	1 2 3	4 5 6	7 8 9
Competency Level	0	I	II	III

THEME 3 SECTION 8:   Respiration/Blood and Circulation

Exercise 8.7 Observing blood cells

Skills indicated by * need to be assessed during the course of the Exercise.

Skill area – Following instructions*

Criteria	Mark	Competency Level
Instructions 1–7 followed *without assistance*. Procedures carried out *competently* and *safely*.	9–7	III
Instructions 1–7 followed and procedures carried out with *occasional assistance*. Shows *awareness* of safety precautions but *sometimes careless*.	6–4	II
Instructions 1–7 followed and procedures carried out only with *regular/constant supervision*. Uses safety precautions *only when reminded*.	3–1	I
Incapable of following instructions 1–7 and carrying out procedures, *or* skill *not attempted*	0	0

Skill area – Manipulation*

Microscope adjustment

Criteria	Mark
Mirror adjusted for optimum clarity	3
Condenser adjusted for optimum clarity	3
Mirror focused for optimum clarity	3

Mark Obtained	0	1 2 3	4 5 6	7 8 9
Competency Level	0	I	II	III

Skill area – Observation*

Criteria	Mark
Drawing identifiable from slide	2
Drawing of reasonable size in terms of space available	2
Relative size of red and white cells correct	1
White and red cells labelled	1
Drawing lines neat, clear, distinct	2
Scale stated (i.e. × 400)	1

Mark Obtained	0	1 2 3	4 5 6	7 8 9
Competency Level	0	I	II	III

THEME 3 SECTION 8: Respiration/Blood and Circulation
Exercise 8.8 Determining blood groups

Skills indicated by * need to be assessed during the course of the Exercise.

Skill area – Following instructions *

Criteria	Mark	Competency Level
Instructions followed *without assistance*. Procedures carried out *competently* and *safely*.	9–7	III
Instructions followed and procedures carried out with *occasional assistance*. Shows *awareness* of safety precautions but *sometimes careless*.	6–4	II
Instructions followed and procedures carried out only with *regular/constant supervision*. Uses safety precautions *only when reminded*.	3–1	I
Incapable of following instructions and carrying out procedures, *or* skill *not attempted*	0	0

THEME 3 SECTION 8: Respiration/Blood and Circulation
Exercise 8.9a Investigating the effect of exercise on pulse rate

Skills indicated by * need to be assessed during the course of the Exercise.

Skill area – Following instructions *

Criteria	Mark	Competency Level
Instructions followed *without assistance*. Procedures carried out *competently* and *safely*.	9–7	III
Instructions followed and procedures carried out with *occasional assistance*. Shows *awareness* of safety precautions but *sometimes careless*.	6–4	II
Instructions followed and procedures carried out only with *regular/constant supervision*. Uses safety precautions *only when reminded*.	3–1	I
Incapable of following instructions and carrying out procedures, *or* skill *not attempted*	0	0

*Skill area – Measurement**

Time

Criteria	Competency Level
Time recorded to within ± 1 second	III
Time recorded outside ± second	0

Skill area – Recording

Results tables

Criteria	Mark
Table 1: 3 counts recorded	1
Mean resting pulse (15 s) recorded	1
Mean resting pulse (1 min) recorded	1
Table 2: 10 counts recorded	1
No anomalous results or anomalous results noted and eliminated	1
Pulse rate per minute recorded for all counts	1

Maximum Competency Level = II

Mark Obtained	0	1 2 3	4 5 6
Competency Level	0	I	II

THEME 3 SECTION 8:   Respiration/Blood and Circulation
Exercise 8.9b   Interpreting the results of Exercise 8.9a

Skills indicated by * need to be assessed during the course of the Exercise.

Skill area – Recording

Graph

Criteria	Mark
Sensible scale	2
Time on x axis	1
x axis labelled *Time (min)*	2
y axis labelled *Pulse rate per min*	1
Points plotted accurately*	1
Points joined accurately*	1
Graph headed	1

*A mark must be obtained for each of these criteria for Competency Level III

Mark Obtained	0	1	2	3	4	5	6	7	8	9
Competency Level	0		I			II			iii	

Skill area – Interpretation

Question	Criteria	Mark
1.	The rate will be higher than the resting rate if any movement has taken place immediately prior to taking the pulse	1
2.	There is a pulse in the thumb	1
3.	To eliminate any inaccuracy which might occur in a single count	1
4.	Glucose and oxygen	2
5. (a)	Pulse rate increases with continued exercise	1
(b)	The faster the muscles contract, the more glucose and oxygen is supplied	1
6.	Oxygen and glucose, used up in muscle contraction, need to be replaced (1). The pulse rate will remain above its resting rate until this replacement has occurred (1)	2

Mark Obtained	0	1	2	3	4	5	6	7	8	9
Competency Level	0		I			II			III	

THEME 3 SECTION 8:   Respiration/Blood and Circulation

Exercise 8.10   The pulse-rate problem – *Experimental design 3*

Skills indicated by * need to be assessed during the course of the Exercise.

Skill area – Experimental design 3

All skills within the skill area *Experimental design* (with the exception of the skill *Recording*) are marked using the following rating scale:

Criteria	Mark	Competency Level
Skill accomplished with no assistance	9–7	III
Skill accomplished with occasional assistance	6–4	II
Skill accomplished with regular assistance	3–1	I
Incapable of accomplishing skill	0	0

Skill – Problem identification/hypothesis formulation

General Criterion: Can identify a problem/formulate a hypothesis.

Specific criteria for this Exercise:
1. (a) Sex (males could have a higher/lower resting pulse rate than females).
   (b) Age (children could have a higher/lower resting pulse rate than adults).
   (c) Size (large/fat people could have a higher/lower resting pulse rate than small/thin people).

2. *Factor – Sex:* Males have a higher/lower resting pulse rate than females of the same age.

   Factor – Age: Children have a higher/lower resting rate than adults.

   Factor – Size: Large/fat people have a higher/lower resting rate than small/thin people of the same age and sex.

Skill – Apparatus selection

General criterion: Can select appropriate apparatus.

Specific criterion for this Exercise: Stop clock/watch. (Essentially, the criterion is the appreciation that only *one* piece of equipment is required.)

Skill – Planning

General criterion: Can produce a logical, staged plan of an experiment with, where appropriate, controls.

Specific criteria for this Exercise: The details will depend on which hypothesis is selected. However, in all cases, the following should apply:

1. Steps 1 and 2, Exercise 8.9a.

2. A comparison of resting pulse rate between 2 stated groups:
   (a) Satisfactory sample of each group taken (e.g. 20).
   (b) Each individual resting pulse rate taken on 3 occasions and the mean obtained.
   (c) Control of variable factors, e.g. a comparison of boys and girls must sample pupils of the same year group.

3. In order to assess a pupil for *Procedure* (below) *some* results need to be obtained during a biology lesson, although this assessment of technique could be based on the previous Exercise (8.9a).

Skill area – Procedure*

1. See 3 above.
2. The results table will indicate whether 2 (a), (b) and (c) above have been taken into account.

Skill – Recording

Resting pulse rate (beats per unit time)									
Group A					Group B				
Sample	Count				Sample	Count			
	1	2	3	Mean		1	2	3	Mean
1					1				
2					2				
3					3				
.					.				
.					.				
.					.				
20					20				

Overall mean resting pulse rate for 20 samples **Group A** =
Overall mean resting pulse rate for 20 samples **Group B** =

Criteria	Mark
Vertical columns headed	1
Horizontal columns headed	1
Pulse rate expressed as beats/unit time	1
Full set of results recorded	1
No anomalous results/anomalous results noted and eliminated	1
Means recorded	1
Results recorded in *single* table	1
Overall layout clear	2

Mark Obtained	0	1 2 3	4 5 6	7 8 9
Competency Level	0	I	II	III

Skill – Interpretation

General criterion: Can reach appropriate conclusions and identify patterns.

Specific criteria for this Exercise: With reference to the results obtained the original hypothesis is confirmed or rejected. If rejected, a new hypothesis is formulated.

Skill – Evaluation

General criteria: Can recognise limitations of method/method improvement/areas of future study.

Specific criteria for this Exercise: Limitations of method – difficulty (a) in locating pulse in very old/very young; (b) in finding suitable *numbers* of samples (e.g. 20 babies, 20 adults over 70 years of age).

Future study: Effect of smoking/diet/obesity on resting pulse rate.

THEME 3 SECTION 9:   Sensitivity and Response

Exercise 9.1   Investigating the sensitivity of organisms using a choice chamber

Skills indicated by * need to be assessed during the course of the Exercise.

Skill area – Following instructions

Criteria	Mark	Competency Level
Instructions followed *without assistance*. Procedures carried out *competently* and *safely*.	9–7	III
Instructions followed and procedures carried out with *occasional assistance*. Shows *awareness* of safety precautions but *sometimes careless*.	6–4	II
Instructions followed and procedures carried out only with *regular/constant supervision*. Uses safety precautions *only when reminded*.	3–1	I
Incapable of following instructions and carrying out procedures, *or* skill *not attempted*	0	0

Skill area – Recording

Constructed table as for Table 1 (Conditions = Dry, Moist/humid)

Criteria	Mark
Vertical columns headed	1
Horizontal columns headed	1
10 results recorded	1
Mean number entered Mean number accurate (whole number) }	1
Results recorded in single table	1
Overall layout clear	1

Maximum Competency Level = II

Mark Obtained	0	1 2 3	4 5 6
Competency Level	0	I	II

THEME 3 SECTION 9:   Sensitivity and Response

Exercise 9.2 Which conditions? – *Experimental design 2*

Skills indicated by * need to be assessed during the course of the Exercise.

Skill area – Experimental design 2

All skills within the skill area *Experimental design* (with the exception of the skill *Recording*) are marked using the following Rating Scale:

Criteria	Mark	Competency Level
Skill accomplished with no assistance	9–7	III
Skill accomplished with occasional assistance	6–4	II
Skill accomplished with regular assistance	3–1	I
Incapable of accomplishing skill	0	0

Skill – Apparatus selection

General criterion: Can select appropriate apparatus.

Specific criteria for this Exercise: As for Exercise 9.1.

Skill – Planning

General criterion: Can produce a logical, staged plan of an experiment.

Specific criteria for this Exercise:

1. Set up Choice Chamber as per Steps 6 and 7 of Exercise 9.1

2. Place black paper over half the choice chamber, as illustrated below:

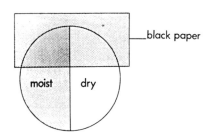

This creates the 4 pairs of conditions under investigation.

3. Set up lamp, 30 cm above Choice Chamber.

4. Place 20 organisms in choice chamber. Record the number of organisms in each quarter of the choice chamber, at 1 minute intervals for 5 minutes. (To record numbers beneath black paper, lift for as short a time as possible and replace.)

The need to replicate the experiment (i.e. use other group's results) should be indicated.

Skill – Procedure*

Specific criterion for this Exercise: Plan (above) followed competently and safely.

Skill – Recording

Table

Conditions	Number of organisms present after:					
	1 min	2 min	3 min	4 min	5 min	Mean
Light/Dry						
Dark/Dry						
Light/Moist						
Dark/Moist						

Criteria	Mark
Vertical columns headed	1
Horizontal columns headed	1
Full set of results recorded	2
Mean numbers recorded	1
Mean numbers recorded accurately to nearest whole number	1
Results recorded in single table	1
Overall layout clear	2

Mark Obtained	0	1 2 3	4 5 6	7 8 9
Competency Level	0	I	II	III

Skill – Interpretation

General criterion for this Exercise: Can reach appropriate conclusions and identify patterns.

Specific criterion for this Exercise: Results used to place preference of organisms in rank order.

THEME 3 SECTION 9:   Sensitivity and Response

Exercise 9.3 Investigating the effect of light intensity on the eye

Skills indicated by * need to be assessed during the course of the Exercise.

Skill area – Observation*

Criteria	Mark
Outline of both drawings the same	1
Drawings of reasonable size in terms of space available	2
Area of iris greater in 2nd drawing Area of pupil less in 2nd drawing	3
Drawing lines neat, clear, distinct	2
Scale stated (e.g. × 1)	1

Mark Obtained	0	1 2 3	4 5 6	7 8 9
Competency Level	0	I	II	III

THEME 3 SECTION 9:   Sensitivity and Response

Exercise 9.4 Investigating the effect of light on the growth of cress plants

Skills indicated by * need to be assessed during the course of the Exercise.

Skill area – Observation*

1. Step 2

Criteria	Mark
Drawings of reasonable size in terms of space available	2

Plants grown in the dark drawn with:
    narrower stems
    longer stems
    smaller leaves
    yellow leaves (labelled)
    drawing lines neat, clear distinct
    scale stated (e.g. × $\frac{1}{2}$)
	1
	1
	1
	1
	2
	1

Mark Obtained	0	1 2 3	4 5 6	7 8 9
Competency Level	0	I	II	III

2. Step 6

Criteria	Mark
Drawings of reasonable size in terms of space available	2
Decapitated seedlings drawn showing no phototrophic response	2
Intact seedlings drawn showing positive phototrophic response	2
Drawing lines neat, clear, distinct	2
Scale stated (e.g. $\times \frac{1}{2}$)	1

Mark Obtained	0	1 2 3	4 5 6	7 8 9
Competency Level	0	I	II	III

Continued

THEME 4 SECTION 10:   Plant Reproduction and Growth

Exercise 10.1   Investigating flower structure and seed production (1)

Skills indicated by * need to be assessed during the course of the Exercise.

Skill area – Following instructions*

Criteria	Mark	Competency Level
Instructions followed *without assistance*. Procedures carried out *competently* and *safely*.	9–7	III
Instructions followed and procedures carried out with *occasional assistance*. Shows *awareness* of safety precautions but *sometimes careless*.	6–4	II
Instructions followed and procedures carried out only with *regular/constant supervision*. Uses safety precautions *only when reminded*.	3–1	I
Incapable of following instructions and carrying out procedures, or skill *not attempted*	0	0

Skill area – Recording

Structure	Number
Sepals	4
Petals	4
Stamens	6

Criteria	Mark
Vertical columns headed	1
Horizontal columns headed	1
3 results recorded	1
Number of sepals, petals, stamens recorded accurately	3
Results recorded in a *single* table	1
Overall layout clear	2

Mark Obtained	0	1	2	3	4	5	6	7	8	9
Competency Level	0		I			II			III	

Skill area – Observation*

1. Stamen

Criteria	Mark
Drawing identifiable from specimen	2
Drawing of reasonable size in terms of space available	1
Filament and anther labelled correctly	1
Pollen grains labelled on anther	2
Drawing lines neat, clear, distinct	2
Scale stated (e.g. × 1)	1

Mark Obtained	0	1 2 3	4 5 6	7 8 9
Competency Level	0	I	II	III

2. Carpel

Criteria	Mark
Drawing identifiable from specimen	2
Drawing of reasonable size in terms of space available	1
Stigma, style, ovule labelled correctly	1
Stigma bilobed	2
Drawing lines neat, clear, distinct	2
Scale stated (e.g. × 1)	1

Mark Obtained	0	1 2 3	4 5 6	7 8 9
Competency Level	0	I	II	III

3. Pod

Criteria	Mark
Drawing identifiable from specimen	2
Drawing of reasonable size in terms of space available	1
Ovules labelled correctly	1
Method of attachment of ovules to ovary wall clearly drawn	2
Drawing lines neat, clear, distinct	2
Scale stated (e.g. × 1)	1

Mark Obtained	0	1 2 3	4 5 6	7 8 9
Competency Level	0	I	II	III

Skill area – Interpretation

Criteria	Mark
Flowers large (1) and brightly coloured (1)	2
Presence of nectar on which insects feed	1
Flower has noticeable scent	1
Stigma/anthers positioned so that an insect's body *must* brush against it/them when searching for nectar	2
New (unpollinated) flowers are produced at the *top* of the flower stalk so they are more accessible to insects	1
Flower faces upwards (1) making it more visible to flying insects (1)	2

Mark Obtained	0	1 2 3	4 5 6	7 8 9
Competency Level	0	I	II	III

THEME 4 SECTION 10:   Plant Reproduction and Growth

Exercise 10.2   Investigating flower structure and seed production (2)

Skills indicated by * need to be assessed during the course of the Exercise.

Skill area – Following instructions*

Criteria	Mark	Competency Level
Instructions followed *without assistance*. Procedures carried out *competently* and *safely*.	9–7	III
Instructions followed and procedures carried out with *occasional assistance*. Shows *awareness* of safety precautions but *sometimes careless*.	6–4	II
Instructions followed and procedures carried out only with *regular/constant supervision*. Uses safety precautions *only when reminded*.	3–1	I
Incapable of following instructions and carrying out procedures, *or* skill *not attempted*	0	0

Skill area – Recording

Structure	Number
Sepals	5
Petals	5
Stamens	10

Criteria	Mark
Vertical columns headed	1
Horizontal columns headed	1
3 results recorded	1
Number of sepals, petals, stamens recorded accurately	3
Results recorded in a *single* table	1
Overall layout clear	2

Mark Obtained	0	1　2　3	4　5　6	7　8　9
Competency Level	0	I	II	III

*Skill area – Observation**

1. Stamen

Criteria	Mark
Drawing identifiable from specimen	2
Drawing of reasonable size in terms of space available	1
Filament and anther labelled correctly	1
Pollen grains labelled on anther	2
Drawing lines neat, clear, distinct	2
Scale stated (e.g. × 1)	1

Mark Obtained	0	1　2　3	4　5　6	7　8　9
Competency Level	0	I	II	III

2. Carpel

Criteria	Mark
Drawing identifiable from specimen	2
Drawing of reasonable size in terms of space available	1
Stigma, style and ovule labelled correctly	1
Bunch of hairs at base of carpel	2
Drawing lines neat, clear, distinct	2
Scale stated (e.g. × 1)	1

Mark Obtained	0	1 2 3	4 5 6	7 8 9
Competency Level	0	I	II	III

3. Pod

Criteria	Mark
Drawing identifiable from specimen	2
Drawing of reasonable size in terms of space available	1
Ovules labelled correctly	1
Method of attachment of ovules to ovary wall clearly drawn	2
Drawing lines neat, clear, distinct	2
Scale stated (e.g. × 1)	1

Mark Obtained	0	1 2 3	4 5 6	7 8 9
Competency Level	0	I	II	III

Skill area – Interpretation

Criteria	Mark
Flowers large (1) and brightly coloured (1)	2
Presence of nectar on which insects feed	1
Flower has prominent scent	1
Stigma/anthers positioned so that an insect's body *must* brush against it/them when searching for nectar	2
New (unpollinated) flowers are produced at the *top* of the flower stalk so they are more accessible to insects	1
Flower constructed so that the insect's body contacts the stigma (1) when it lands on the 'platform' of petals (1)	2

Mark Obtained	0	1 2 3	4 5 6	7 8 9
Competency Level	0	I	II	III

THEME 4 SECTION 10:   Plant Reproduction and Growth
Exercise 10.3 Investigating the structure of a wind-pollinated flower

Skills indicated by * need to be assessed during the course of the Exercise.

Skill area – Interpretation

Question	Criteria	Mark
1. (a)	Green	1
(b)	Flowers not very noticeable (1). Absence of bright colours could cause insects to ignore them (1)	2
2.	Anthers held outside the flower (1) and hang loosely so they are easily blown by the wind (1)	2
3.	Stigmas large and 'feathery' (1). This provides a large surface area for 'catching' wind-borne pollen grains (1)	2
4.	Wind-pollination is more random/less certain than insect-pollination, so more pollen has to be produced	1
5.	Small, smooth pollen grains are light and easily wind-borne	1

Mark Obtained	0	1 2 3	4 5 6	7 8 9
Competency Level	0	I	II	III

THEME 4 SECTION 10:   Plant Reproduction and Growth
Exercise 10.4 Investigating the structure and development (germination) of pollen grains

Skills indicated by * need to be assessed during the course of the Exercise.

Skill area – Observation *

Criteria	Mark
Drawings identifiable from slides	2
Drawings of reasonable size in terms of space available	1
Some surface detail drawn of pollen grains in A	1
Pollen tube(s) drawn, accurately in B	2
Drawing lines neat, clear, distinct	2
Scale stated (e.g. × 200)	1

Mark Obtained	0	1 2 3	4 5 6	7 8 9
Competency Level	0	I	II	III

Skill area – Manipulation*

Microscope adjustment

Criteria	Mark
Mirror adjusted for optimum clarity	3
Condenser adjusted for optimum clarity	3
Microscope focused for optimum clarity	3

Mark Obtained	0	1 2 3	4 5 6	7 8 9
Competency Level	0	I	II	III

THEME 4 SECTION 10: Plant Reproduction and Growth
Exercise 10.5 Investigating seed dispersal

Skills indicated by * need to be assessed during the course of the Exercise.

Skill area – Observation*

Criteria	Mark
Seeds/seed-containing structures allocated to correct groups ($\frac{1}{2}$ mark each)	5
Wind-dispersed seeds: structures for increasing surface areas	1
Bird-dispersed seeds: seeds surrounded by fleshy fruit	1
Mammal dispersed seeds: seeds/seed-containing structures have hooks	1
Explosive-dispersed seeds: seeds contained in pods	1

Mark Obtained	0	1 2 3	4 5 6	7 8 9
Competency Level	0	I	II	III

THEME 4 SECTION 10:   Plant Reproduction and Growth

Exercise 10.6 Investigating the structure of a seed and its food reserves

Skills indicated by * need to be assessed during the course of the Exercise.

*Skill area – Observation**

1. Table

Criteria		Mark
Dry seed	**Soaked seed**	
Testa hard	Testa soft	2
Testa firmly attached	Testa loosely attached	2
Testa wrinkled (broad bean) } Testa mottled (French bean) }	Testa smooth (broad bean) } Testa not mottled (French bean) }	2
Seed shrunken	Seed swollen	2
Water enters through small hole below the scar		1

Mark Obtained	0	1 2 3	4 5 6	7 8 9
Competency Level	0	I	II	III

2. Drawings

Criteria	Mark
Drawings identifiable from specimen	2
Drawings of reasonable size in terms of space available	2
Plumule/radicle drawn (labelling *not* required)	2
Drawing lines neat, clear, distinct	2
Scale stated (e.g. × 1)	1

Mark Obtained	0	1 2 3	4 5 6	7 8 9
Competency Level	0	I	II	III

Skill area – Manipulation*

Step 6

Criteria	Mark
Bunsen remains alight throughout test	1
Low, blue flame maintained	1
Flame controlled using air hole and gas tap	1
Sensible technique for cooling water if temperature rises above 40°C (e.g. add cold water)	1

Frequent temperature checks:
    with thermometer *in* the water
    but raised off base of beaker
	1
	1
	1

Temperature of water maintained between 35°C and 40°C throughout the test	2

Mark Obtained	0	1 2 3	4 5 6	7 8 9
Competency Level	0	I	II	III

Skill area – Recording

Results table

Test reagent	Result	Nutrient present
Iodine solution		
Benedict's solution		
Biuret reagent		

Criteria	Mark
Vertical columns headed	1
Horizontal columns headed	1
3 results recorded	1
End-point colours accurately described	2
Nutrient(s) present recorded	1
Results recorded in *single* table	1
Overall layout clear	2

Mark Obtained	0	1 2 3	4 5 6	7 8 9
Competency Level	0	I	II	III

THEME 4 SECTION 10:   Plant Reproduction and Growth

Exercise 10.7a   Investigating what happens to the starch in a germinating seed

Skills indicated by * need to be assessed during the course of the Exercise.

Skill area – Following instructions*

Criteria	Mark	Competency Level
Instructions followed *without assistance*. Procedures carried out *competently* and *safely*.	9–7	III
Instructions followed and procedures carried out with *occasional assistance*. Shows *awareness* of safety precautions but *sometimes careless*.	6–4	II
Instructions followed and procedures carried out only with *regular/constant supervision*. Uses safety precautions *only when reminded*.	3–1	I
Incapable of following instructions and carrying out procedures, *or* skill *not attempted*	0	0

Skill area – Observation*

Step 6

Criteria	Mark
Drawing identifiable from petri dish	1
Drawing of same size as that for Steps 2 and 3	2
Orientation of drawing the same as that for Steps 2 and 3	1

Stained/unstained regions:
    drawn accurately
    labelled or indicated by colour or key
	1
	1

Drawing lines neat, clear, distinct	2
Scale stated (e.g. $\times \frac{1}{2}$)	1

Mark Obtained	0	1 2 3	4 5 6	7 8 9
Competency Level	0	I	II	III

THEME 4 SECTION 10:   Plant Reproduction and Growth

Exercise 10.7b   Interpreting the results of Exercise 10.7a

Skills indicated by * need to be assessed during the course of the Exercise.

Skill area – Interpretation

Question	Criteria	Mark
1. (a) (b) (c)	Starch present No starch present Under and around the unboiled seed (B)	1 1 1
2.	Enzyme/amylase/carbohdrase	2
3.	Changed to sugar/maltose	1
4.	Enzyme destroyed (denatured) by boiling	1
5.	Sugar used in cell respiration (1) to provide energy for making new cells (1)	2

Mark Obtained	0	1 2 3	4 5 6	7 8 9
Competency Level	0	I	II	III

THEME 4 SECTION 10:   Plant Reproduction and Growth

Exercise 10.8   The germination problem – *Experimental design 3*

Skills indicated by * need to be assessed during the course of the Exercise.

Skill area – Experimental design 3

All skills within the skill area *Experimental design* (with the exception of the skill *Recording*) are marked using the following rating scale:

Criteria	Mark	Competency Level
Skill accomplished with no assistance	9–7	III
Skill accomplished with occasional assistance	6–4	II
Skill accomplished with regular assistance	3–1	I
Incapable of accomplishing skill	0	0

Skill – Problem identification/hypothesis formulation

General criterion: Can identify a problem/formulate an hypothesis.

Specific criteria for this Exercise:

1. Oxygen
2. Air
3. Is Oxygen (in the air) necessary for the germination of cress plant seeds?
4. Oxygen is needed for the germination of cress plant seeds.

Skill – Apparatus selection

General criterion: Can select appropriate apparatus.

Specific criteria for this Exercise:

Apparatus required: Boiling tubes   Boiling tube rack
Bunsen burner   Oil
Test tube holder   Cress seeds
Bungs   Black paper/aluminium foil
Chinagraph pencil   Spatula
Hand lens

Skill – Planning

General criterion: Can produce a logical, staged plan of an experiment with, where appropriate, controls.

Specific criteria for this Exercise:

1. Divide cress seeds into 2 equal batches. Label 2 boiling tubes A and B.

2. Fill each boiling tube one-third full of water.

3. Boil the water in tube A to remove the oxygen. Allow to cool.

4. Place a batch of seeds into the water in each boiling tube.

5. Pour a layer of oil on to surface of water in A (prevent entry of atmospheric oxygen).

6. Put bungs into each boiling tube and cover each tube with black paper/aluminium foil (simulate natural conditions).

7. Shake tube B, daily, to aerate.

8. Leave both tubes for *stated* period of time (e.g. 5 days) in warm conditions.

9. After stated time check (a) number of seeds in each tube, and (b) number germinated in each tube (using hand lens).

10. Calculate percentage germination in each tube.

   Criterion for germination should be stated (e.g. emergence of radicle).

Skill – Procedure*

Specific criteria for this Exercise: Can follow plan (above) competently.

Skill – Recording

Specific criteria for this Exercise:

Results table

Batch	Number of seeds present	Number of seeds germinated	Percentage germination
A (minus O_2)			
B (plus O_2)			

Criteria	Mark
Vertical columns headed	1
Horizontal columns headed	1
Full set of results recorded	1
% germination tabulated	1
% germination calculated correctly	2
Results recorded in *single* table	1
Overall layout clear	2

Mark Obtained	0	1 2 3	4 5 6	7 8 9
Competency Level	0	I	II	III

Skill – Interpretation

General criterion: Can reach appropriate conclusions and identify patterns.

Specific criteria for this Exercise: A comparison of the percentage germination in tubes A and B will lead to an acceptance or rejection of the hypothesis. If rejected, a new hypothesis is formulated.

Skill – Evaluation

General criterion: Can recognise limitations of method/method improvement/areas of future study.

Specific criteria for this Exercise:

7. Limitations of method: water in tube A not boiled long enough; not allowed to cool sufficiently before adding seeds; tube B not aerated; difficulty in determining whether a seed has germinated.

8. Clay soil must be well aerated/treated to increase aeration for maximum germination.

9. Can *large* seeds (e.g. peas, beans) germinate better than cress seeds in an oxygen deficient soil?

THEME 4 SECTION 10: Plant Reproduction and Growth

Exercise 10.9 Investigating the growth of the stem of a French bean plant

Skills indicated by * need to be assessed during the course of the Exercise.

Skill area – Following instructions*

Criteria	Mark	Competency Level
Steps 1–6 followed *without assistance*. Procedures carried out *competently* and *safely*.	9–7	III
Steps 1–6 followed and procedures carried out with *occasional assistance*. Shows *awareness* of safety precautions but *sometimes careless*.	6–4	II
Steps 1–6 followed and procedures carried out only with *regular/ constant supervision*. Uses safety precautions *only when reminded*.	3–1	I
Incapable of following instructions and carrying out procedures, *or* skill *not attempted*	0	0

Skill area – Measurement*

(As the measurements are taken over a period of 4–5 weeks, each candidate can be assessed for this skill area three times.)

Criteria	Competency Level
3 measurements accurate to ± 1 mm	III
2 out of 3 measurements accurate to ± 1 mm	II
1 out of 3 measurements accurate to ± 1 mm	I

Skill area – Recording

NB Both graphs marked using same Criteria.

Criteria	Mark
Sensible scale	2
Time, on x axis, labelled *days*	2
y axis labelled *length/height (mm)*	2
Points plotted accurately*	1
Points joined accurately*	1
Graph given a suitable title	1

*A mark *must* be obtained for each of these criteria for Competency Level III.

Mark Obtained	0	1	2	3	4	5	6	7	8	9
Competency Level	0		I			II			III	

NB Questions 1–6 not for assessment.

THEME 4 SECTION 10:   Plant Reproduction and Growth
Exercise 10.10   Investigating the growth of leaves of a French bean plant

Skills indicated by * need to be assessed during the course of the Exercise.

Skill area – Following instructions*

Criteria	Mark	Competency Level
Steps 1–6 followed *without assistance*. Procedures carried out *competently* and *safely*.	9–7	III
Steps 1–6 followed and procedures carried out with *occasional assistance*. Shows *awareness* of safety precautions but *sometimes careless*.	6–4	II
Steps 1–6 followed and procedures carried out only with *regular/ constant supervision*. Uses safety precautions *only when reminded*.	3–1	I
Incapable of following instructions and carrying out procedures, or skill *not attempted*	0	0

Skill area – Measurement*

NB As the measurements are taken over a period of 4–5 weeks, each candidate can be assessed for this skill area three times.

Criteria	Competency Level
3 areas recorded accurate to ± 2%	III
3 areas recorded accurate to ± 5%	II
3 areas recorded accurate to ± 10%	I

Skill area – Recording

Graph

Criteria	Mark
Sensible scale	2
Time, on x axis, labelled *days*	2
y axis labelled *area (mm²)*	2
Points plotted accurately*	1
Points joined accurately*	1
Graph given a suitable title	1

*A mark *must* be obtained for each of these criteria for Competency Level III.

Mark Obtained	0	1 2 3	4 5 6	7 8 9
Competency Level	0	I	II	III

NB Questions 1 and 2 not for assessment.

THEME 4 SECTION 10:   Plant Reproduction and Growth
Exercise 10.11   Investigating variation in width of privet leaves

Skills indicated by * need to be assessed during the course of the Exercise.

Skill area – Measurement*

Length

Criteria	Competency Level
3 measurements accurate to ± 1 mm	III
2 out of 3 measurements accurate to ± 1 mm	II
1 out of 3 measurements accurate to ± 1 mm	I

Skill area – Recording 1

1. Written tally

Criteria	Competency Level
Recording a written tally accomplished with:	
No assistance	III
Occasional assistance	II
Regular assistance	I
Skill not attempted	0

2. Graph

Criteria	Mark
Sensible scale	2
Width of leaf on x axis, expressed in *mm*	2
Measurements on x axis (e.g. 11–14) ascribed to *columns*	1
y axis labelled *Number*	1
Bars plotted accurately*	2
Graph given a suitable title	1

*A mark *must* be obtained for this criterion for Competency Level III.

Mark Obtained	0	1 2 3	4 5 6	7 8 9
Competency Level	0	I	II	III

Question (not for assessment): Any sensible, stated environmental factor – e.g. shade/light.

Appendix I

Supervisor's Check Lists

1. Following instructions, Measurement, Manipulation, Observation

Exercise No. _____   Exercise _____

Teaching Group _____   Date _____

Teacher _____

Skill Area / Candidate	Following instructions		Measurement	Manipulation	Observation

Continued

Exercise No. _____   Exercise _____

Teaching Group _____   Date _____

Teacher _____

Skill Area / Candidate	Following instructions		Measurement	Manipulation	Observation

NB TO BE USED DURING PRACTICAL ASSESSMENTS FOR RECORDING PART MARKS/TOTAL MARKS/COMPETENCY LEVELS

2. Experimental design

Exercise No. _____   Exercise _____

Teaching Group _____   Date _____

Teacher _____

Competency level attained for the following Skills:																					
Skill \\ Candidate	*Problem ident./hyp. formulation*			*Apparatus selection*			*Planning*			*Procedure*			*Recording*			*Interpreta-tion*			*Evaluation*		
	III	II	I	III	II	I	III	II	I	III	II	I	III	II	I	III	II	I	III	II	I

Continued

Exercise No. _____   Exercise _____

Teaching Group _____   Date _____

Teacher _____

Competency level attained for the following Skills:																					
Skill	Problem ident./hyp. formulation			Apparatus selection			Planning			Procedure			Recording			Interpreta-tion			Evaluation		
Candidate	III	II	I	III	II	I	III	II	I	III	II	I	III	II	I	III	II	I	III	II	I

Appendix II

Candidate's Record of Assessment

Name _____   Teacher _____   Examining Group _____

Skill area	Skill*	Exercise No.	Date	Competency Level
Following instructions				
Manipulation				
Measurement				
Observation				
Recording				
Interpretation				
Experimental design				

* REQUIRED BY THE EXAMINING GROUP FOR ASSESSMENT (TO BE FILLED IN BY SUPERVISOR)